Talking to Children about Divorce

Talking to Children about Divorce

A Parent's Guide to
Healthy Communication
at Each Stage of Divorce

JEAN MCBRIDE, MS, LMFT

ALTHEA
PRESS

*For our children and
their courageous parents*

Contents

4 Having the Talk 53

5 Children's Reactions and Worries 76

If you've found your way to this book, it likely means that divorce has touched your life. Whether you're just beginning the process or if you have been working through it for a while, you may be looking for support or guidance to help you and your children navigate this emotional minefield. You probably want to know how to initiate those crucial but hard-to-have conversations and how best to answer your children's questions. Most importantly, you want reassurance that your children are going to be okay through your divorce and as you rebuild a life after.

How do I know this? I've been a marriage and family therapist specializing in divorce and remarriage for over 25 years. In 1994 I developed a court-ordered class for divorcing parents in Colorado that I still teach. It has been my honor to work with thousands of families going through divorce. Each one has helped me better understand what parents and children require to emerge from divorce in the healthiest way possible.

On a personal note, when my son was six years old, his father and I divorced. Having been there myself, I have a good idea of what keeps you awake at night, with your stomach churning and your thoughts racing. My son's father and I managed to have an amicable divorce and keep our son out of the conflict. To be honest, it was more by luck than anything else. I would have loved to have a book like this one to guide me.

As parents, we never want to hurt or disappoint our children, and yet we know that in most cases, the decision to divorce will do just that. We can't imagine how in the world to tell them, or how any of us will get through it. But I did, and you will too. It *is* possible to take a path through divorce that doesn't create shame, fear, blame, and anger as toxic byproducts. The actions are simple, but not always easy. The benefits, though, are huge: healthy, happy, well-adjusted children.

I remember eight-year-old Jason, whose parents brought him to see me because he was having nightmares and his behavior was changing. As he sat in my office playing with toy cars, he told me his mother couldn't possibly love him because he looked just like his dad. His thinking: If Mom doesn't love Dad anymore and I look just like him, how can she love me? His parents were shocked that their son had put these two thoughts together. I helped them find specific words and actions to reassure Jason that they loved him no matter what. Fairly quickly, Jason was able to relax, his behavior improved, his nightmares went away, and he genuinely understood that his parents loved him dearly. As you might guess, this wasn't an easy conversation for the adults but it was one that was critical for Jason. Knowing what to say enabled Jason's parents to turn the corner for their son. Likewise, by understanding what to say to your children, you can help them learn to be resilient and bounce back from difficult experiences. As divorced parents, our goal is to create an environment of love, support, and absolute security that allows our children to rise above the bumps and bruises that our divorce, and really all of life, hands them.

In this book I will:

- Walk you through concrete actions you can take to help your children weather the emotions of divorce.

- Give you exact words to use in a variety of situations that commonly arise.

- Teach you simple actions you can take every day that will improve communication both with your former spouse and your children, ease your children's stress, and help them feel safe and secure.

- Explore the most current research about divorce and help you apply it to your own family.

If you're ready to make a difference for your children, read on. I'll be here with you, offering my help, tools, encouragement, and perhaps an occasional prod to keep you moving forward. Together, we'll do it.

JEAN MCBRIDE, MS, LMFT

1

CHAPTER

Developing Healthy Communication Habits

Before we get into the details of talking with your children about divorce, let's set the stage for successful communication in general. In this chapter, we'll discuss what goes into effective communication, how to maintain quality parenting through divorce, and ways to keep your children from feeling caught between two people they love. We'll also look at how to manage anger and protect your children from any adult conflict that may arise. Finally, we'll discuss what effective co-parenting (short for "cooperative parenting") entails and offer 10 tips for co-parenting success.

The Power of Language

At the end of a class I teach for divorcing parents, I always ask two questions: "What is your biggest concern about divorce?" and, "What is your main takeaway from this class?" The majority of parents give the same answer every time: communication. And they're right. Divorced parents often must be better at communicating with each other than they were when they were married. Good communication skills smooth out day-to-day interactions and keep discussions of tricky topics from getting out of hand.

Choosing Your Words

Let's start with some word choice basics. When talking about the other parent with your children, use their role. For example, "Jeremy, your dad will be here in 10 minutes." Or, "This is your weekend to be with Mommy." When speaking to someone other than your children about the other parent, use their role or their name, like this: "Lisa's mom will be picking her up after soccer practice." Or, "We've traded weekends so the kids can spend time with Frank's parents when they're in town."

Many divorced people use "my ex" when referring to the other parent. While this has become common, avoid it. You may be an ex-spouse, but neither of you will ever be an ex-parent; your word choice can telegraph that to your children and others. Finally, it may seem obvious but avoid derogatory names for the other parent, even if you think your kids won't hear you. It puts you in a disrespectful mindset, and if by chance your children do overhear your unkind words, they're likely to feel hurt.

Your Tone and Body Language

Good communication skills go beyond the words we choose. Body language and tone can enhance your message or detract from it. Children are experts at reading body language and assessing tone, so be aware of what you're putting out there. Tone of voice, for instance, goes a long way in conveying your true message. Think about the phrase, "Your dad's on the phone." By using similar words or simply changing your tone, you can make a negative, snarky statement ("Ugh. Your dad is calling again.") or a positive one ("Honey, Dad wants to chat with you.") Your children are tuned in to your tone as much as to the actual words you use.

Similarly, there are many nonverbal cues that could alter the intent of the phrase, "Your mom is going to be a few minutes late." If you roll your eyes, shake your head, or make a face, your negative message is clear, no matter what words you use. If you smile, soften your voice, and give a reassuring touch, it's an entirely different message. In what you say and how you say it, the choice to be positive or negative is always yours.

Being the Best Parent You Can Be

People in the midst of divorce often use weather metaphors to describe their experience: a tornado, hurricane, tsunami, or a raging river overflowing its banks. All depict something out of control, overwhelming, frightening, and life threatening. From the middle of this emotional maelstrom, how can parents continue the day-to-day tasks of caring for their children? How will you and your children weather this storm?

First, and perhaps most importantly, know this: All storms pass. You and your children will get through it. You can still be the excellent parent you strive to be. Your challenge is to remain actively engaged with your children while you disengage from your marriage. This is no easy task because of the many feelings such as anger, grief, sadness, and loneliness that often accompany divorce. If we return to the metaphor of the raging river, feelings are the huge boulders and tree limbs that seem to appear with no warning, threatening to impede your progress or overturn your boat. They're unpredictable and frightening. But take heart. On this river, and in divorce, there are a number of steps you can take every day to ensure that you and your children make it through safely.

STAY INVOLVED

When going through a divorce, it's tempting to withdraw from parenting. You may feel guilty for initiating the divorce or adding to the conflict. Sometimes you're simply worn out and exhausted emotionally and physically. You may think it's hard enough to take care of yourself, let alone your children. But withdrawing isn't an option if you want your children to thrive. They need both parents. Make it your priority to know what's important to them by checking in on school and activities, spending time together, and getting to know their friends. Likewise, encourage and support the other parent's active involvement in your children's lives. This is not the time to limit access to your children. They need both of you.

CREATE TWO CHILD-CENTERED HOMES

Your children will need their own space to feel at home with you. If you will be living in a new place, designate a room for them and let them help equip it. If a room isn't possible, set aside a closet, dresser, or bookshelf just for them. Do everything you can to make it their home.

MAINTAIN ROUTINES

Children thrive on routine. Even though your life has changed, maintain their daily routines. Honor school and extracurricular commitments. Follow established meal and bedtime schedules. Keep meaningful family traditions, though perhaps celebrating in new ways. For instance, instead of trying to recreate your usual family Thanksgiving gathering, start a new tradition such as hiking and an outdoor picnic, volunteering at a soup kitchen, or staying in pajamas and playing board games all day.

SET HEALTHY EXPECTATIONS AND BOUNDARIES

Families are stronger and your children will feel more secure when you have clear expectations of each other; when the rules and boundaries are understood and seen as fair; and when everyone knows how they are expected to contribute to the family.

MAKE YOURSELF AVAILABLE

More than ever, your children need you as your family adjusts to your new lives. Stay close to home when they are with you. Hanging out together to watch a movie or play games are good options. Make family mealtimes a priority. Slow down, unplug, and be willing to listen to what they have to say—even the difficult things. A good guideline: Listen more than you speak.

REMAIN IN THE ROLE OF THE ADULT

Don't use your children as sounding boards for your problems or feelings, no matter how sensitive or sympathetic they may be. It's important for them not to become your confidante because it thrusts them into more adult information than they can handle, encourages them to take sides, and often creates anxiety and fear. Find appropriate adult support systems, like friends or family, so that you aren't tempted to let your children take on the role.

Putting Children First

Think of your children for a moment. What do you want for them? What kind of life will you give them? These are crucial questions to consider as you work through divorce and life afterward. Most parents want the best for their children and want to know the divorce isn't going to harm them. For that to be so, you must do one thing without fail: Put your children first. Day by day, every choice, thought, and word must go through this filter: Will it help or hurt my children?

It may sound daunting and even impossible. It is a big task—big and necessary. The research is clear: Divorced parents who put their children's emotional and physical needs ahead of their own have healthier, happier, better-adjusted children. In divorce, parents must love their children more than they dislike or disagree with their former spouse. Here's how to put your children first:

- Protect them from parental conflict.
- Create child-oriented schedules.
- Listen without judgment.
- Encourage regular access to both parents.
- Don't ask them to choose between parents.
- Create two stable, child-centered homes.
- Maintain predictable, consistent routines with minimal disruptions.
- Encourage children to be children.
- Let children know that both parents love them.
- Provide a safe, loving environment.
- Emphasize that they aren't responsible for the divorce.
- Use a warm, authoritative parenting style.

Managing Anger and Conflict

Going through divorce and creating a life afterward based on the agreements in your parenting plan is like riding a roller coaster of emotions. One minute you feel like everything is going fine and the next you're on the verge of a meltdown. This is normal. It's how most everyone getting divorced feels: up/down, high/low, happy/sad, calm/angry, and sane/crazy. The dismantling of a marriage brings up emotions you may not even know you have. You're raw, and every feeling is more intense. You may find yourself wanting to blow up at your children's other parent, being overly critical, or getting into power struggles. You may use anger to justify the divorce, create distance, or simply to vent. You may feel terribly hurt by the other parent's actions. You may feel sad, depressed, rejected, humiliated, hopeless, or frightened. In this stew of toxic emotions, anger feels like an understandable reaction. You're hurting and want to lash out.

But here's the thing: Parental conflict is the biggest predictor of poor outcome for children. *The biggest.* The more frequent and intense the conflict between you and your former spouse, the harder it is on your kids. And if the arguments are about the child specifically, the outcome is worse still. As difficult as it can be, keeping your anger in check and shielding your children from conflict are vitally important. These strategies will help.

CARVE OUT A CONFLICT-FREE ZONE AROUND YOUR CHILDREN

Make a commitment to avoid exposing children to your arguments. Yes, there will be times when this seems impossible, maybe because the other parent won't cooperate or because you feel like you've just had it. Hang in there. Remind yourself why keeping your kids free from conflict matters. You can limit conflict by setting and respecting boundaries; having a clear, complete parenting schedule and following it; refusing to be baited into a fight; and taking responsibility for your actions. Other ways to conflict-proof your communications include thinking twice before sending an angry or accusatory text or email, adopting a businesslike tone when dealing with the other parent, and dealing with just one issue at a time.

GET SUPPORT

Feelings have a way of taking over unless you tend to them. Talk with trusted friends, schedule time with a licensed therapist, attend a divorce support group, and learn tools to manage anger. There are many wonderful books, websites, and programs to help. Check out the resource section at the end of this book for suggestions. You don't have to handle your feelings alone.

PRACTICE HEALTHY, NONVIOLENT COMMUNICATION WITH AND ABOUT THE OTHER PARENT

Cultivate compassion for yourself, your children, and your co-parent. Divorce is difficult and emotionally exhausting for everyone. Most of the time, everyone is simply doing the best they can. Anger usually turns into more anger because each time we say something negative, it becomes more familiar and easier to do the next time. The same is true when we say kind and compassionate things. Pat yourself on the back when you do well and give yourself a break when you don't.

TAKE GOOD CARE OF YOURSELF

You'll handle the stresses of divorce better with good self-care. This is the time for some true TLC (tender loving care). Exercise, eat nutritious food, and get enough sleep. Schedule time with friends, spend time outdoors, allow yourself to slow down, and look inward through activities such as deep breathing, yoga, meditation, or journaling.

10 Ways to Succeed at Co-Parenting

Effective co-parents respect each other, communicate in an amicable way, and focus on their children's needs. Learning to co-parent takes time and practice. You will stumble over your communication attempts, let your feelings get in the way, forget an agreement you made, or show up late for something. You'll lose your temper or blame the other parent. In these moments, be easy with yourself and with your co-parent. Take a few deep breaths, smile, and focus on your intent to cooperate. Then try again. These strategies will help:

1. **Get yourself to a positive place.** You'll be better able to help your children adjust to the many changes divorce brings when you've tended to yourself first. Do the emotional work necessary to heal from your divorce. Get enough sleep, eat healthy food, and exercise. If you feel depressed, anxious, or overly angry, find a licensed therapist and/or a divorce support group to help you work through the feelings.

2. **Make decisions based on your child filter.** One of my clients is a divorced father and he tells me that he runs every decision he makes and every action he takes through his "Danielle filter." When he doesn't feel particularly cooperative, or has the urge to get back at his former spouse for something she did, he remembers his daughter Danielle and considers what's in her best interest.

3. **Consult the other parent when making decisions about your children.** In a successful co-parenting relationship, both parents will have input about their children. Sometimes one parent will be the designated decision maker. Still, it is important and respectful to bring the other parent into the discussion. It will strengthen your co-parenting relationship and help your children.

4. **Respect each other as parents.** Even though your relationship as marital partners is ending, your role as parents will never change. Seeing the other parent's value and respecting his or her active involvement in your children's lives will help you succeed as a co-parent.

5. **Support and encourage the other parent's presence in your children's lives.** Allow room for the other parent to actively participate. Do your part to make transitions easy and drama-free. Accept that you don't have to always agree. The other parent will have good ideas and insight about the children you share. Be open to them.

6. **Separate your emotional relationship from your co-parenting relationship.** Keep your feelings about the other parent and your life together separate from your ability to co-parent.

7. **Communicate directly with the other parent.** Never ask children to carry messages between parents or report on what happens at the other parent's home. Something you think is a fair request could spark an angry reply from the other parent—and the messenger will be left to deal with it.

❯

8. **Share information with the other parent.** Co-parenting is like installing a giant safety net under your children so that if they stumble or fall, one or both of you will be there to catch them. If you have information about your child, tell the other parent. Say, for example, your son is upset after school because another boy was teasing him on the playground. Even if you talked it through and your son feels better, give the other parent a heads-up in case it happens again during his or her parenting time. When both parents are "in the loop," the safety net remains strong and your children benefit.

9. **Abide by your financial agreements.** Trust is a key factor in effective co-parenting. One important way to build and maintain trust is to respectfully handle the money that goes between you. Pay child support and/or other financial commitments on time. If you receive child support, use it wisely.

10. **Help your children easily move their belongings between homes.** Rise above petty squabbles about where the smartphone, bicycle, or clothing must stay. Never hold your children's belongings hostage by not allowing them to go to the other parent's home. Accept the fact that children will forget things and practice a gracious, calm attitude as you help them retrieve what they need from the other parent's home.

Keeping Kids Out of the Middle

Once you decide to divorce, what's usually best for adults is to end the relationship and no longer see the other person. Children, however, need to maintain an ongoing relationship with both parents. This means that having your former spouse out of your life completely is not an option. The two of you can make the situation less stressful for your kids by ensuring that they never feel caught between the two people they love most. I'll be honest. This can be a big challenge even for parents who mean well. An offhand sarcastic comment, subtle pressure to agree, or tension whenever parents are together can all cause stress for kids.

So, you're probably wondering, how can parents really keep their children out of the middle? These dos and don'ts will help:

- **Do** be careful to never to ask your children to choose between the two of you or take sides in a disagreement.

- **Don't** ask your children to keep secrets from the other parent.

- **Do** choose your words carefully to avoid bad-mouthing the other parent in front of your children.

- **Don't** ask your children to speak badly about the other parent.

- **Do** keep discussions of parenting business such as financial and legal matters strictly between you and the other parent.

- **Don't** ask your children to relay messages between parents or for information about the other parent.

- **Do** give the other parent the benefit of the doubt instead of assuming the worst.

- **Do** take the high road and refuse to respond to remarks the other parent makes about you.

- **Don't** argue in front of the children.

If you're wondering what it looks like for a child to be caught in the middle, consider this story:

Ten-year-old Cara's dad found her taking money from his nightstand. When he asked her about it she replied, "Mom doesn't have enough money to buy food because she says you won't give her any." Cara's father was outraged and accused her mother of lying. "I'm calling her right now. She lies all the time. Don't trust anything she says," he raged.

Cara spent the rest of the night in her room, worrying that she had caused a big problem between her parents. When she got back to her mother's house, she was unusually quiet. Her mother asked what was wrong. "Dad says you're a liar and I shouldn't trust you," Cara replied. Now it was Mom's turn to be furious. "How dare he say that? I'm calling my attorney. You're not going back there until he apologizes," she said.

In this case, Cara got caught between her parents in an argument over which she had no control. Child support is an issue for adults to handle. Plus, calling each other a liar and threatening to withhold parenting time hurts Cara terribly because she loves both of her parents.

Separating from Your Spouse, Not Your Kids

Divorce is one of the most stressful events in a person's life, second only to the death of a spouse. The longer you've been together, the harder it is to make the emotional and physical separation, even when you know things are no longer working. Rather than being one event, divorce tends to be a series of changes and adjustments that typically lasts anywhere from one to three years and sometimes even longer. During this time, you have the challenge of gaining distance and emotional disengagement from your former spouse while remaining actively involved with your children. This is complicated because what's typically best for adults in divorce is not best for children and vice versa.

What Children Need

From the stressful, unsettling days when it first becomes clear the marriage is ending, through the process of divorce, and finally through acclimating to separate homes and changed lives, children need both of their parents more than ever. This is the time to increase your availability, not reduce it or disappear altogether. It's also important to stick with familiar daily routines, rules, and expectations. You'll need to provide children with a sense of safety in an environment where everything else is changing.

If you're the parent who has moved from the family home, staying involved takes planning as well as support and cooperation from your co-parent. We'll talk more about this in chapter 7. If you are the parent with whom your children live most of the time, smooth the path for other parent to stay involved. Though it may be tempting to avoid the other parent as you deal with your own feelings, make the effort to keep the other parent connected for your kids' sake.

What Adults Need

In the exhausting process of divorce there are hundreds of details, large and small, that require your attention. For you and your children, nearly every aspect of life changes. You may be living in a new place, starting a new job, and handling responsibilities that your former spouse used to manage. This is disorienting and at times completely overwhelming. Like children, adults benefit from getting settled into a safe, comfortable living space and re-establishing familiar routines. Making this a priority will be a comfort to both you and your children.

A key difference between you and your children is that while you should maintain their relationship with your former spouse, your task is to disengage from him or her and the life you had together so you can begin to rebuild a separate, post-divorce life. To do this successfully, I offer two strategies. First, rewrite the rules of your relationship. Now is the time to establish a new way of interacting within clearly defined boundaries. Your only point of intersection is your children. The other parent's private life is no longer your concern. In the beginning, it may be difficult to step away from knowing everything about each other's lives. With time and intention, it will get easier.

The other thing you need to do is to start thinking of your relationship as a business partnership in which your children are your joint enterprise. You're no longer in a romantic relationship nor are you simply friends. You are business partners and as such standard business protocol will serve you well. Be respectful and polite, stick to an agenda when you have items to discuss, communicate clearly, abide by agreements you make, listen to the other parent's ideas, and be willing to negotiate. Like true business partners, sometimes you will simply have to agree to disagree.

Leaning on Your Family Support System

As you and your children adjust to your new way of being a family, it may be tempting to isolate yourselves because you feel over-whelmed or embarrassed. Resist this urge. The American Family

Assets Study, carried out by the Search Institute in Minneapolis, identified key qualities that help strengthen all families. One asset, what they called "connecting to community," tells us that both adults and children fare best when they maintain strong connections to family, friends, and neighbors.

We've all heard the saying, "It takes a village to raise a child"; well, now is the time to activate the members of your village. Tell teachers, coaches, and school counselors about the divorce so they can be prepared to best support your children. Use familiar babysitters and stick with your children's long-time medical and dental providers, as well as other professionals if circumstances allow. Continue at least some of your children's favorite activities: sports, music, and hobbies, for example. Stay in touch with grandparents and extended family members. Don't ask your family to take sides but allow and encourage their involvement with your children. Just as your children need both of you and their other parent to thrive, they also need the freedom to know and love everyone in their family.

If you've moved as a result of the divorce, schedule play dates with friends from the old neighborhood or school. If face-to-face visits aren't feasible, use technology to maintain the connections. If you're in a new neighborhood, make it a point to meet your neighbors and participate in events and activities. The sooner you get to know people, the sooner your new environment will feel like home.

2

CHAPTER

Getting Kids to Open Up

In the last chapter we talked about the power of communication and ways that you can use words and body language to manage anger, be a successful co-parent, and set up your children for success as you go through the process of divorce. Now let's delve into the ways that you can encourage productive communication with your children. From making enough time to talk to them to listening without judging, there are several strategies you can use to help and comfort your kids.

Divorce doesn't end a family, but instead gives it a new form. Children now have two homes instead of one, with two sets of rules and expectations. And while you and your former spouse no longer live together, you must stay actively engaged as parents for your children to thrive. In some ways, parenting after divorce takes more skill than when you were together, especially when it comes to communicating with and about your children. As you rebuild your life and work to help your children adjust to this new style of being a family, what you say and do will make all the difference.

Scheduling One-on-One Time

Each of your children is going to need regular time alone with you. It's a basic human need to be seen and valued as an individual, and it is more important than ever for your children as they navigate your divorce.

As a single parent, you have a tremendous number of demands on your time and energy, so prioritizing one-on-one time with each child will take some creative thinking. However, you should make the effort because it will pay off big-time for your children. Your attention will help each child feel special and important to you and give them an opportunity to seek your reassurance on issues that may be troubling them. Keep in mind that one-on-one time doesn't have to take all day to be effective. In fact, being fully present with your child for even a short time does wonders. Turn off your phone, limit interruptions, and make eye contact. Here are a few ways to sneak in some valuable talk time with your children:

MAKE GOOD USE OF CAR TRIPS

Conversations on the way to an appointment, activity, or to and from school can turn into wonderfully satisfying interactions.

ENACT A "STAY UP LATER" POLICY

One child will get to stay up later than siblings for special time with you. Rotate the privilege among children so everyone gets a chance.

PLAN PARENT/CHILD DATES

Find time to share an occasional dinner or special activity with each child. Go on a bike ride, get ice cream, or attend a school function together. Choose activities that require interaction and facilitate conversation.

TUNE IN TO EACH CHILD'S SPECIAL INTERESTS

Do an art project together, take care of a beloved pet, listen with appreciation to her music practice, read together, or play with favorite toys. The point isn't what you do, it's that you do something meaningful with your child.

GIVE EACH CHILD A TURN AS "HELPER OF THE DAY"

Enlist your children to assist you with basic chores, from planting a garden to cooking a meal to raking leaves together. Your task has to be enjoyable for the child, not something he sees as a punishment.

Listening without Judging

Have you noticed how much easier it is to listen when you like what's being said? And when we don't like what we're hearing, listening without reacting is hard. Fair warning here: You are not always going to like what your children have to say about the divorce. You may feel uncomfortable, defensive, embarrassed, or even ashamed. But it's so very important to listen and learn exactly how they feel. If you want your kids to talk openly with you, you must learn to listen more than you speak. Someone once quipped that's why we have two ears and only one mouth!

Once your children are comfortable enough to tell you how they feel, the surest way to dampen their enthusiasm is to criticize what they say. If you listen without judgment, you'll avoid these spirit-crushing comments:

- "What's wrong with you?"
- "Stop acting like a baby."
- "Quit crying."
- "You are not [insert feeling word]."
- "You sound just like your mom/dad."
- "That's the stupidest thing I've ever heard."
- "Tone down the drama."
- "You just don't understand."
- "Sit still and pay attention."

You get the picture. Using words that belittle, criticize, or judge will shut down the flow of conversation in an instant. These toxic words also contribute to children's feelings of low self-compassion, lack of confidence, and hopelessness.

In contrast, when you create an atmosphere of acceptance and willingness to hear everything, even the tough stuff, your children will trust you enough to respond with authenticity. These nonjudgmental phrases will help:

- "Tell me more."

- "I see."

- "Oh? Hmm. Really?"

- "What was that like?"

As you can see, sometimes you don't have to say much. Your attentive, interested expression and open body language may be all the invitation your child needs to open up. Even a friendly nod can keep the discussion going.

Listening with Empathy

When we respond to our children with empathy it means we are doing our best to understand their feelings. We put ourselves in their shoes to see things from their vantage point. When we seek to understand their experience, our children feel supported. We validate their feelings and give credence to what they're telling us. Empathic listening empowers children to figure things out.

The difficult part: Empathy doesn't always come so easily. To truly listen with empathy we must let go of any agenda we may have. For instance, we may want our child to stop feeling sad and secretly hope that by listening we can convince her to see that things aren't as bad as she thinks. Our agenda is about what we're hoping to accomplish, rather than what she's feeling. However, our real task is to pay total attention and listen with an open heart. Listening with empathy is not offering advice or trying to influence. It's simply listening with the intention to understand. Sometimes it's called reflective listening.

Say you talk with your six-year-old about the fact you're getting a divorce. At the end of your talk he throws a toy car across the room, and screams, "I hate you!" How do you listen with empathy?

PARENT *Looks like you're pretty mad right now.*

CHILD I said I hate you.

PARENT *I see. You're very angry with me.*

CHILD Yeah, I'm angry. *(Wipes a tear from cheek)*

PARENT *You're so angry it's making you cry.*

CHILD *(Nods a yes)*

PARENT *You didn't like this talk about divorce?*

CHILD I don't want to move to another house.

PARENT *Mmm. I can see how that would be upsetting.*

CHILD What if I don't have my things when I'm at your new house?

PARENT *You really want to know you'll have everything you need at my house?*

CHILD Yes. I want my cars and racetrack.

PARENT *You love playing with your cars.*

CHILD *(Smiling slightly)* Next I'm going to make a loop for the cars to go around.

PARENT *You have big plans for your cars and you don't want our divorce to get in the way.*

CHILD Yeah. Can I bring my cars to your new house?

PARENT *Yes. In fact, how about we take a few with us on Sunday when we go see the house?*

CHILD Okay.

What this conversation has just done is help the child acknowledge and name his fear (that he won't have his much-loved cars to play with at a new house) and help his parent understand his angry response to the divorce talk. By not punishing him for getting angry and throwing the car, the parent was able to help the child calm down. Together they found a solution that comforted the child. When a child says, "I hate you," it's tempting to tell him he doesn't mean it or punish him for being disrespectful. Neither of those responses would help him feel heard or solve the problem.

Cultivating and Conveying Hope

In talking with hundreds of children, I've learned that one of their worst fears is that their parents will get a divorce. Even the word scares them, like the bogeyman is coming for a visit. For parents, it can be the same. Fear of the unknown is powerful and frightening. Divorce changes every single aspect of a family's life, and the chaos that often accompanies it can be overwhelming.

Among the many tasks parents must tackle to help children thrive through the divorce, one of the most important is to give them hope. In words and actions, your children must receive this message again and again: "We're going to be just fine." Or, "We will always take care of you." Or, "It's going to be okay. Maybe a little different at first, but we'll get through this."

The challenge is that parents often don't believe it themselves. They get stuck in their own emotions, feeling discouraged and hopeless. And from that low point, it feels nearly impossible to be hopeful, let alone share the message with children. My advice: To borrow a phrase from Alcoholics Anonymous, "Fake it until you make it." Each day, find at least one thing to be grateful for. Help your children do the same. Keep putting one foot in front of the other, no matter how tired or hopeless you feel. Taking action will fuel your hope.

Many studies have found that divorce doesn't have to be the doom and gloom that people assume it is. My own experience working with families has shown this too. Negative outcomes *can* be reversed. In fact, by following the suggestions in this book to protect your children from conflict, remain actively engaged as their parents, reassure them of your steadfast love, and help them understand and talk about their feelings, you will give them a positive emotional jumpstart. Always cultivate hope.

Interpreting the Signals Your Child Is Sending

We don't always know what our children are feeling. The fact is that we don't always know what *we* feel. Talking about emotions is like speaking a foreign language for many adults. When we compound this lack of skill with the terrible hurt, sadness, grief, guilt, shame, and embarrassment that often accompany divorce, it's no wonder we don't know what to say or do. Instead we take the ostrich approach, sticking our head in the sand and denying that we have feelings at all. "If we don't talk about them, they aren't a big deal," we tell ourselves. We may even believe that . . . until our children's distress breaks us out of our denial.

Masking True Feelings

Children can be masters at keeping their true feelings under wraps, especially when it comes to something as emotionally charged as divorce. Parents must patiently learn to speak their children's special language, to listen between the lines to begin to understand the real feelings. Unless they've had parents who are exceptionally good at teaching them about emotions, children often don't have the words to accurately describe their feelings.

Why might children hide feelings in the first place? As a parent, you probably think you're open to hearing everything about your kids' feelings. But I want to challenge you a little on this. Sometimes what we want to hear are the good feelings, the ones we like and believe reflect well on us. We aren't as open to hearing the negative feelings, the ones that make us uncomfortable. Have you ever tried to modify or censor your child's feelings with one of these?

- "Slow down and tell me what really happened."

- "Don't use that word. It's not nice."

- "You certainly do not feel that way, young man."

- "I'm not going to talk with you until you've calmed down."

- "You're just saying that because you're tired."

- "There's no reason to be so upset."

These statements deny children's feelings and over time erode their confidence in knowing what they feel. But when parents really listen and acknowledge the pain under their children's words, they build a bridge for their children to trust that they know what they know. When they don't think they have to cover up their true feelings, children become less upset and better able to name and understand all of their feelings.

In his book *Raising an Emotionally Intelligent Child,* John Gottman, PhD, uses the term "emotion coaches" for parents who help their children understand feelings. Emotion coaches don't back away from intense feelings but use them as learning opportunities. They teach their children strategies to navigate life's ups and downs. Gottman and his colleagues have identified five steps in the process of emotion coaching:

1. Pay attention to the emotion.

2. Recognize it as a teaching opportunity.

3. Listen with empathy as you validate what your child feels.

4. Help your child label the emotion.

5. Explore strategies to solve the problem.

Here's a look at those steps in practice. In a whiny voice, your eight-year-old daughter tells you she wishes she were back at Dad's house. You're hurt but you focus on her feelings. You listen carefully and reflect back to her what she says, helping her to name the emotion. "Daddy had a headache when he brought you here and you're worried about him." If you're correct, you'll get an affirmative reply—a nod or a "yes" or look of relief. Then you can begin to explore a solution. "Would you like to give Daddy a call to make sure he's feeling better?"

Using the practices of an emotion coach will encourage your children to openly express their feelings about the divorce and really any area of life. Dr. Gottman's research has found emotion coaching to be a proven protection from the emotional trauma of divorce.

Understanding Body Language

Our body language is an outward reflection of what we're feeling on the inside. Paying attention to the nonverbal cues that our children give us is the first step to finding out what's upsetting them.

With young children, it usually doesn't usually take high-powered observation skills to understand their body language. Angry, sad, or happy facial expressions, loud voices, over-the-top silly behavior, throwing things, hitting or kicking, and sticking out a tongue now and then, all send clear messages about feelings. Likewise, when younger children isolate themselves from the family or friends, have trouble sleeping, or regress to behaviors from an earlier developmental stage, parents usually pick up these signals that something is not quite right.

Older children tend to be less obvious, making adults work a bit harder to figure out what's troubling them. Though parents of teens can observe angry outbursts, slammed doors, eye rolling, sighing or snorting, and defiantly crossed arms, it may be harder to determine the cause. In some cases, a body language cue doesn't match the words being said. For example, a concerned parent might say to a teen, "You seem upset. Is everything okay?" The teen responds with a glare and the words, "I'm fine."

So which is it? Are they angry about something, or are they fine? The words say one thing while the body language expresses something quite different. It takes a persistent, attentive parent to first notice the behavioral cues, and then use openhearted, nonjudgmental listening to get to the true feelings. Earlier I gave you an example of listening with empathy to a young child. Here's how doing so with a teen could play out.

SAMPLE SCRIPT

PARENT *You seem upset. Is everything okay?*
TEEN   I'm fine. *(Said with attitude)*

PARENT *Your expression and tone of voice don't say fine.*
TEEN   Well, I am fine.

PARENT	*Hmm.*
TEEN	What?
PARENT	*I'm just noticing that you look upset.*
TEEN	Your questions are making me upset.
PARENT	*You're tired of me asking how you are.*
TEEN	Yeah.
PARENT	*Okay. Just know that I care and am here if you want to talk.*
TEEN	Mom!
PARENT	*Got it. No more questions right now.*

While this conversation didn't answer the parent's question, it demonstrates two things. First, the teen knows his parent is paying attention and genuinely cares. Second, it models a way to respectfully introduce the topic and then accept the boundary the teen sets.

A final word of advice: Don't take your child's body language personally. All forms of communication are important. Think of those angry looks, crossed arms, and grunted responses as golden opportunities to explore emotions and develop more intimate communication. Research shows that children whose parents coach them to express and understand their emotions fare better than children whose parents don't provide such guidance. They fare better on a number of measures: physical health, social skills, violent behavior, school performance, and resilience.

3

CHAPTER

Preparing for the Talk

The purpose of "the talk" is to let your children know your plans to divorce and what will happen in their lives. When you and your co-parent prepare for this conversation and agree on what you'll tell your children, it will be more comfortable for everyone. This chapter will help you plan the logistics, such as when and where the talk will take place. We'll also cover how to discuss the parenting plan you're working out. First, though, we'll tackle the tricky topic of whether or not to let your children know your marriage isn't working even before you've finalized the decision to divorce.

Early Warnings

One of the most common questions I am asked is, "Should parents tell children about the problems in their marriage?" followed by, "If so, what's appropriate to share?" Thinking about this issue often keeps parents awake until the wee hours. Their worry is understandable because how much to share with your children about problems in your marriage is complicated territory.

In chapter 1, we introduced the importance of protecting children from adult conflict. As I said, it's simply not healthy for them to witness their parents' arguments or to be drawn into the details. That said, if fighting is intense and/or frequent, chances are the children are already well aware of the marital problems. In these cases, the divorce will probably come as no surprise to them. Interestingly, research shows that in high-conflict families, children may view the divorce more positively because they believe the day-to-day arguments will stop. Sadly, some parents carry their conflict beyond the end of the marriage and into parenting after divorce, but we'll talk more about that later.

In other families, parents keep their marital problems hidden from their children. If that's the situation in your home, you may want to consider pulling back the curtain just a little. When children believe everything in their world is perfect, they can be completely blindsided by the news of a divorce. This can lead to feelings of betrayal and a sense that their parents have fooled them. As a result, children begin to doubt themselves and their observations.

As far as how much to tell children, parents always walk the tightrope of giving just enough information without getting into inappropriate details or turning the conversation into an argument. You could say something like, "Dad and I have been having some problems getting along. We're talking a lot and getting help from a counselor. But we just aren't as happy being married as we used to be."

This is no easy conversation, and introducing the idea that there are problems will definitely put your children on high alert. In fact, there's always the possibility that your kids will come out and ask if you're planning to get a divorce. If your talk is just to warn them that things are not going well, then answer honestly that you don't know yet. Even if there are still unknowns, there may be some benefits to offering a heads-up, suggests Robert Emery, PhD, in his book, *The Truth about Children and Divorce*. First, his research shows that giving children notice about their parents' marriage problems can serve as a kind of inoculation against more stress. Having this knowledge allows children to later focus on their feelings and the many changes divorce brings without having to also deal with the life-shattering discovery that their happy family has been a lie. If the divorce never happens, children still gain an important life lesson: Even good marriages can have problems. Emery also suggests that this early warning talk gives children an overall more realistic view of life. Naturally, as parents, we want only the best for our children, but it's important for them to learn that every family can have hard times. It helps develop empathy and compassion—both important life skills.

Come Prepared with a Parenting Plan

Before sitting down to talk with your children, you should have a parenting plan in place. In the best scenario, you and your co-parent will work this out together. If that's not possible, perhaps because you live far from each other or because you can't be in the same room without arguing, then sit down and draw up a plan on your own. This isn't the time to wing it. Be prepared to tell your children as many of the details as possible. Announcing the separation/divorce without offering specifics could launch your children into an emotional free fall, fueled by their own fears and misinformation.

The finalized parenting plan you and your co-parent develop should address most of the logistical issues. When you first tell your children about the divorce, it will comfort them to have answers for these common questions:

WHERE WILL MOM LIVE? WHERE WILL DAD LIVE?

Be specific. If you are the parent moving, describe your new home and schedule a time to look at it with the children. This is true even if your new home is a tiny apartment, a room with friends, your parents' basement, or a hotel. Your children need to see where you'll be.

WHERE AM I GOING TO LIVE?

If you already have a temporary parenting plan worked out, share it. Don't leave children wondering. If you know your current plan will change in the future, say so. For instance, "For now you'll be living here, but also spending some time with Mom. As we figure things out, the schedule could change a little. But don't worry. We'll always let you know before a change will happen." Then describe *exactly* what "spending some time with Mom" means. For example, "Mom will pick you up from school every Tuesday and Thursday. You'll have dinner with her and stay at her house until 7:30 when I take you back to my house. And you'll spend all day Saturday and Saturday night at Mom's house."

WHERE WILL MY PET LIVE?

Children worry about their animals. In some divorce situations they must give up a favorite pet. Be sensitive to their feelings and include planning for the family pets.

WILL I GO TO THE SAME SCHOOL?

Predictability creates emotional safety for children. At first, if you are able to do so, limit changes in their neighborhood and school or day care. As children adjust to the divorce, you can begin to introduce some change.

WHEN WILL I GET TO SEE MY DAD (OR MOM)?

Tell your children that you're working on a schedule that will be good for everyone. Describe what you've agreed on for the immediate future. "We're still working on a plan, but right now here's how we'll see each other and how you'll see Dad." It helps young children to have a visual reminder of when they'll be with each parent. Explain that you'll help them choose stickers or special colors to represent each parent and use them to mark the calendar with each parent's time. Older children and teens will also benefit from having a calendar with the specifics clearly marked.

Have a Temporary Plan If Necessary

At the time of your talk, you may not yet have worked out a parenting plan. It can be an emotional and complicated process that many parents don't start until after they've separated. If this is true for your family, you will need a temporary plan that addresses your children's questions. Come up with something short term so they know how and when they will see each of you. Here again, a calendar that clearly shows which days will be spent with each parent can be helpful.

Keep in mind that having even a temporary plan is critical for your children. Without one, it can become easy for days or weeks to pass without seeing your children. Don't let precious parent–child relationships become a casualty of the emotionally exhausting and chaotic early days of separation and divorce. For everyone's sake, make a plan and follow it. Keep cancellations or changes to a minimum. Being able to count on seeing each parent on a predictable schedule will help your children adjust to this huge change in their lives.

Do We Really Need a Plan?

Every now and then I hear from parents who don't want a parenting plan. They believe they can work together well enough without committing things to paper. Here's my concern with this: Children do best when they know when and how they'll see each parent. There are simply too many variables that could go wrong without a plan to keep everyone on track.

One little girl I worked with comes to mind. Because her parents didn't have a written plan, there was some miscommunication about which weekend her dad was picking her up for a visit. On the weekend she and her mother expected him, the girl sat on her front porch, her backpack beside her, waiting for her dad. He didn't come because he thought his parenting time was the following weekend. She'd been looking forward to seeing him all week, and she was devastated and felt abandoned by him even though her mother explained the mix-up. This is why I feel separating without a plan is like trying to build a house without architectural plans; it's something most of us wouldn't attempt. The details and structure are that crucial.

That said, if you have an extremely amicable co-parenting relationship, you and your former spouse can always make small changes to your agreed-upon parenting plan. For example, you might want to increase parenting time or change how you handle holidays and other special occasions. But following a basic plan will keep your children's lives running smoothly. Any changes you do make, perhaps allowing for spontaneous outings or attending extra school activities, can be happy bonuses. As long as both parents agree and there is no conflict, almost anything goes. Just remember to always view the arrangements you make from the lens of what your children need, not what you want.

Who Should Be Present

Since the purpose of this talk is to let your children know about the divorce and help them understand and begin to deal with their feelings, it's important to set it up to be comfortable for them. You are the experts on your children and have a good idea about what will work best. Here are some things to consider as you plan who will be present.

One Parent or Two

This talk will always be less stressful and more comforting for your children when both parents are present. While it may be uncomfortable for you to be in the same room with the other parent, remember the purpose of the talk is to help your children understand what will be happening in their lives. It is completely about what they need rather than what you want. Throughout the process of divorcing, a helpful mantra is this: "What's best for my children? What actions can I take right now that will help them?"

Telling children together helps them understand that this is a joint decision where no one is to blame. If, in reality, the divorce isn't a joint decision, but one that has been forced on you, it's still in your children's best interests to suggest that you arrived at the decision together. Anything else puts them into the uncomfortable position of knowing too much about adult problems. They may feel obligated to take sides or assign blame, neither of which is good for children. Another benefit: Delivering the message jointly demonstrates a united parenting front and keeps adults in their important role as parents and leaders of the family, even as it is changing form. It also ensures that children hear the same message, rather than one version from Mom and another from Dad.

The only situation where it is not recommended that both parents be in the room to talk with the children is when adults are likely to act disrespectfully toward each other or escalate the discussion into an argument. Because exposing children to parental conflict is never good, separate talks are the way to go. If the discussion starts out well, but tensions rise and an argument is likely to erupt as you get going, make the choice to stop the discussion and pick it up at another time when everyone is feeling calmer.

Siblings Together or Separate

The logistics of this talk can change considerably based on the number of children in a family. Parents wonder whether to gather all their children together or to meet with them in separate groups based on age. Generally speaking, if there is a wide variance in ages—say a three-year-old and a thirteen-year-old—separate conversations will best meet each child's needs. When you are able to tailor what you say and how you say it to your children's ages, the conversation will go much smoother. Younger children require a short, simple explanation. Older children are able to participate in longer talks and often will ask in-depth questions that require complex answers. Holding separate discussions with children of similar developmental abilities and/or chronological ages will help you address all of your children's needs. You'll find some sample scripts for these different conversations in chapter 4.

When to Tell the Kids

The timing of your announcement is as important as what you'll say about the divorce. You'll be discussing a sensitive topic that will bring up strong feelings for all of you. Planning when and how to best carry it out will help you calm any anxiety you may feel about telling your children this hard-to-hear news and gives you a structure to follow in what is often a very chaotic time.

The first timing issue is how much notice to give before one of you moves out of the house. Depending on their ages, your children will need differing lengths of advance warning. With young children, preschoolers to preteens, my recommendation is to tell them no more than two weeks prior to a parent moving out of the family home. Anything shorter can leave them stressed and overwhelmed, as if things are moving too fast. Anything longer encourages false hope that the divorce won't happen. Teenagers are better able to understand the situation and can handle learning about the separation and divorce up to a month or so before it happens.

The second timing consideration is choosing the actual day and time for your conversation. Here are some things to think about:

BE READY

Choose a time to talk when you feel emotionally prepared. Come with a clear head—no alcohol or drugs for false courage. Stick to a script. Don't blurt out the news just to get it out of the way.

TELL CHILDREN FIRST

Respect your children enough to tell them before you tell others. This is especially important if there is a chance that they could hear the news from someone other than you, like a friend or family member. This is hard news to receive and getting it secondhand makes it even more painful.

CHOOSE AN HOUR OF THE DAY WHEN YOU ARE REFRESHED

Stay away from late nights, early mornings, or discussions before bedtime, heading to school, or when you're about to leave for work.

CHOOSE A TIME WHEN YOUR CHILDREN CAN CONCENTRATE

Do your best to avoid times when children are sick, distracted by other events, tired, or hungry.

ALLOW PLENTY OF TIME

Give your children all the time they need to take in this big information. Be open and willing to hear what they have to say and ask if they have any questions or want to say anything.

BE MINDFUL OF SCHEDULES

Avoid important dates like holidays, birthdays, the first day of school, or the first day of summer vacation to name a few. This talk will stay embedded in your children's brains long into adulthood. Try not to link a special occasion to this very emotional experience.

WATCH OUT FOR "HIT AND RUN TALKS"

I coined this term after hearing many stories of parents gathering their children to tell them about the divorce, and then disappearing immediately afterward. The parents would drop a bombshell and then be completely unavailable to a child who might have a question or just need a hug. Schedule your conversation for a time when you're available to stick around afterward. Your presence will provide comfort, even if your children retreat to their rooms.

NO ADVANCE WARNINGS

Telling your children ahead of time that you are going to have a talk about divorce will only increase their anxiety. Simply announce the meeting as you are heading into it.

Things to Avoid in Your Talk

You are about to tell your children that everything they've known and counted on in their family is changing. This is not the time to ask them to agree with your decision or otherwise make you feel better. This talk is for them. To make your conversation as low-stress and productive as possible, stay child-focused. These tips can help:

Avoid interruptions. Turn off all screens: no phones, tablets, computers, or television. Set up a welcoming, emotionally safe environment.

No tattling. This isn't the time to divulge sensitive details about why your marriage isn't working or to try and get the children on "your side." In fact, there isn't ever an appropriate time for this.

Stay away from trash talk about each other. This conversation is going to be hard enough on your children. Subjecting them to a verbal bashing session between their parents will only make it much worse. Be respectful and businesslike.

Watch your body language. Children will read your nonverbal cues as well as the words you use. Try to avoid sitting like an emotionless robot or a volcano about to explode. Make your facial expressions mirror your words. And no smirking, eye rolling, sarcasm, or put-downs.

No runaway emotions. It's good to share your feelings with your children. You may find your voice cracking or tears clouding your eyes as you speak. This is normal and perfectly fine because it helps your children understand how difficult this decision is for you. However, uncontrollable weeping or over-the-top emotional outbursts will frighten your children and make them think they must take care of your emotions rather than their own.

Don't play the blame game. Don't identify one parent as responsible for the divorce. It's better to say that you've made the decision together, and that no one is the "bad guy."

Sidestep the "L-word." When you tell your children you no longer love the other parent, it leaves them worried that you'll stop loving them too. Even gentle, tactful explanations about the differences between adult love and parental love can be confusing. It's much more effective to describe how the relationship has changed. For example, "We argue a lot," or, "We don't agree on many things," or, "We're no longer happy being married to each other." While these can still be confusing, children understand arguments and unhappiness much easier than trying to figure out falling out of love.

Where to Have the Talk

As you plan the setting for your talk with your children, think about what *they* will need. Choose a location that is familiar, private, and emotionally safe.

FAMILIAR

Your children will probably feel most comfortable in their home. You might sit in the living room or around the kitchen table. Sometimes parents will request the discussion be held at a therapist's office. This only works if the children know and feel comfortable with the therapist. Never schedule an appointment with someone who doesn't know how to facilitate this talk.

PRIVATE

This is a conversation that needs privacy. There are likely to be tears or emotional outbursts that could embarrass a child if overheard. These are normal reactions that we don't want to suppress. Choose a place where you won't be interrupted or worry about who might be listening. This isn't a conversation for a restaurant or other public location. Respect your children's feelings and give them the privacy they need.

EMOTIONALLY SAFE

Familiarity and privacy will go a long way toward helping your children feel safe enough to participate in this emotionally difficult conversation. You should also use what you know about each of your children to meet their individual needs for emotional safety. For some kids this might mean they feel safest when it's just the two of you with your child curled up on your lap on the family room couch, while others might feel safest in their bedroom but want their siblings present.

4

CHAPTER

Having the Talk

You know your children best and are the expert when it comes to parenting them. Think of sitting down with them to talk about the divorce as an important gift from you. Interestingly, research has shown that very few parents make the time to do this. They worry that talking about the divorce will make children feel worse. This fear is understandable because as parents we are reluctant to tell children something that will hurt them. Yet not doing it will hurt them even more, because not understanding what's happening will lead to fear and uncertainty. Also, keep in mind that there is almost never only one big talk. You are much more likely to participate in a series of smaller talks as your children work through what this life change means.

The Big Message

Before we get into the words you will use, I want to emphasize there is really a vital two-part message your children must hear from you again and again. This is the core of everything you will say to them. It may take a variety of forms, with different words for each situation. Your children may need you to repeat it for weeks, months, and in some cases, years.

Here is part one: *Your children must know and believe that the divorce will never change your love for them, and you will always be their parents and take care of them.* This alone is a big message, but there's more to it. Part two is that your actions—the things you do and say each and every day—have to back your message 100 percent. To borrow a familiar phrase, you must walk your talk.

We may think of love as a feeling, but more than that it's a verb—an action verb. Children feel loved through your actions as well as your words. Follow the parenting schedule, show up for their activities, shield them from conflict or hostility between you and their other parent, listen with respect to their questions and concerns, keep them out of the middle, allow them to be children rather than burden them with adult responsibilities, have fun with them, and repeatedly tell them how much you love them. When you put their needs first, they will deeply and appreciatively get your message.

Enacting this two-part message, what I call the "gold-plated guarantee" of your abiding love and presence in their lives, gets children through this big change with as little trauma as possible. It will support their emotional and physical development. It will soothe and comfort them when things aren't going well. It will give them wings to fly when they are ready.

Providing this guarantee may seem like the easiest thing in the world or the hardest. Either way, it will take your complete intention, focus, and willingness to put your children first. Parenting is a process that will last through your lifetime in one form or another. Getting divorced ends a marriage, not your role as parents.

Tune In to Body Language

As you talk with your children about the divorce, in this first conversation and the many that will follow, pay attention to body language—yours and theirs. Body language can be a powerful external expression of what we're feeling, and yet many of us are totally unaware of it.

Researchers have identified nearly a million nonverbal cues and signals that we use to communicate. These include the way we hold our bodies and use our hands, our facial expressions, breathing and throat sounds, our posture, the way we hold our mouth, and eye contact, to name only a few. The ability to read emotions is hardwired into us. Perhaps you've had the experience of meeting someone for the first time and knowing exactly how she felt about you from nothing more than her facial expression. We usually know when people are paying attention to us and when they are blowing us off. We can sense friends versus enemies and danger versus safety.

Paying attention to the emotional signals you're sending and noticing the cues your children are giving you can transmit valuable information. Here are a few ways to use body language to encourage a productive conversation with your children:

- Take care to match your body language to the tone and content of your words.
- Get down on your child's eye level when speaking.

- Make eye contact but don't stare them down.

- Lean slightly toward your child as you listen.

- Offer a reassuring touch or hug. Hold young children in your lap.

- Nod, smile, and make soothing sounds while your child is speaking.

Three Types of Divorce

How you and your child's other parent interact will determine in part the way you talk with your children as well as your parenting style after the divorce. Robert Emery, PhD, in his book *The Truth about Children and Divorce*, suggests that divorces fall into three categories: cooperative, angry, and distant. The descriptions below will help you identify your style. Don't feel that it's a contest where everyone must have a cooperative divorce. It's great if you do, but in the real world sometimes cooperation simply isn't possible. Rest assured there are ways to effectively parent after divorce within each of these categories.

The Cooperative Divorce

Cooperative parents tend to instinctively know how to put their children's needs above their own because it is a continuation of how they've been parenting all along. They tend to be better tuned in to their children. As an example, cooperative parents are likely to understand how an occasional adjustment to the parenting plan to include more time with one parent would benefit their children. In a cooperative divorce, parents are fairly good at communicating with each other about their children, working out an amicable parenting plan, and generally keeping life running smoothly.

Cooperative parents will likely talk with their children about the divorce together. Since parents who fall into this category tend to keep their marital problems private from their children for as long as possible, learning of the divorce may be surprising for children. It will be important to share feelings of sadness or disappointment about the marriage not working and to encourage children to express their feelings.

WHAT TO DO

- Be certain the divorce will happen before you tell your children.

- Have a plan about where everyone will live and how the children will see each of you.

- Tell the children together.

- Share your feelings. It's okay and even healthy to let your children know you are also sad and disappointed that the marriage is ending.

- Be affectionate with your children.

- Listen more than you speak.

- Follow-up later to encourage your children to ask any questions that they think of after they digest the information in your talk.

WHAT TO SAY

When you've tried to make your marriage work and to protect your children from the hard things in life, this talk is especially painful for you—and yet very important for your children. No sample script will get it completely right for your family. You'll have to make the adjustments to fit your situation, but here's a good place to start:

MOM *We have something important to tell you about a change in our family. Daddy and I haven't been getting along very well lately. We have some adult problems we haven't been able to fix, even though we've tried. We don't want to be married to each other anymore.*

DAD *I know this must be very hard to hear. It makes us sad, but it's something Mom and I agree on. We're getting a divorce. That means we aren't going to live together or be married anymore. In a couple of weeks I'm going to move to a new house where you'll have your own rooms just like now. On Sunday, if you like, I'll take you to see it.*

CHILD Where will you live Mommy?

MOM *I'll stay in this house. Daddy and I are working out a schedule so you'll spend time here with me and some time with Daddy at his new home. We want you to know this is not your fault. We will always be your mom and dad and take the best care of you that we can. We love you more than anything. That will never change.*

DAD *That's right. Divorce is something grown-ups do. It's never about children. Mommy and I will always love you and be your parents. Do you have questions?*

CHILD Do I have to go to a different school?

MOM *Oh yes, that's a great question. Nothing about school will change. You'll still be able to see all your friends and participate in gymnastics and soccer.*

DAD *We know this is a big change. We're going to do our best to make sure your life stays pretty normal. Come to us anytime with any questions you have.*

The Angry Divorce

Sometimes one or both parents are so hurt by things that have damaged the marriage that they are unable to feel anything but anger. They act out their feelings through lack of cooperation, power struggles, and attempts to get back at each other. With this level of conflict, parents are often unable to step away from their pain to accurately see their children's feelings. Instead they try to draw their children into the conflict, encouraging them to take sides and distance themselves from the other parent. Nothing is more toxic to children.

Numerous studies confirm that exposing children to parental conflict is the biggest predictor of poor outcome. School performance, physical health, emotional health, the ability to get along with peers, and adult relationships are influenced negatively by living with parents who cannot manage conflict. Raging at one another in front of the children is like force-feeding them a spoonful of poison each time. It's that damaging.

If you are in an angry divorce, there are steps you must take to help your children: first, deal with your anger. You may need the help of a therapist to examine what's going on, and then begin to fix it. Second, cloak your children in an invisible protection barrier by never again putting them in the path of your anger toward their other parent. That means you watch what you say and do every time you're with your children. Yes, this is hard but it is crucial.

In high-conflict families, the news of divorce usually comes as no surprise to children. They see firsthand that the marriage isn't working and often are relieved when the fighting ends. If you are unable to be in a room with your child's other parent without anger, plan separate talks with your children.

WHAT TO DO

- If possible, work out a basic parenting agreement before you talk with the children.

- Talk with your children separately.

- Speak for yourself.

- Share your feelings without bad-mouthing the other parent.

- Listen to your children's concerns.

WHAT TO SAY

This script can get you started as you think about what to say to your children when they are aware of the anger between you and their other parent. Even in situations of high conflict, it is best to keep your explanations simple.

SAMPLE SCRIPT

PARENT   *Your dad and I have been having lots of arguments. I'm sorry you had to hear them. I bet it scared you.*

(Pause for the response)

PARENT   *We've tried to work things out, but we haven't been able to. We're getting a divorce. This means we aren't going to live together or be married anymore. But we will always be your mom and dad. We're working out a plan where you can spend time with Dad and time with me. For now, you'll live here with me during the week and go to Dad's on Saturday and Sunday. It makes me really sad but your dad and I think it's best for us. It isn't your fault in any way. Something that will never change is how much we love you.*

PARENT   *This is a lot of really big information. Do you want to ask me anything?*

(Wait for reply)

PARENT   *It's okay if you don't. We have plenty of time to talk about it whenever you want. Dad and I are always going to take care of you. Only now you'll have two houses instead of one.*

(Big hug or hand squeeze)

The Distant Divorce

In a distant divorce, parents tend to be more emotionally detached from each other than in a cooperative or angry divorce. Distance usually has defined the marriage as well as the divorce, with very little emotional exchange between the adults. In distant marriages, children aren't exposed to parental arguments, which is good, but they also don't see loving interactions. When the news about the divorce comes, it may or may not be a surprise to the children.

When talking with children about their divorce, distant parents must still abide by the gold-plated guarantee: Children must know they are not to blame, that they are loved, and that their parents will always be there for them.

WHAT TO DO

- Be affectionate with your children.
- Share your feelings. Show your sadness or disappointment.
- Protect your children from your anger.
- Ask for questions and offer child-appropriate answers.
- Follow up later.

The sample scripts from the cooperative divorce and the angry divorce will work well for the distant divorce. Depending on the level of conflict at the time, parents can deliver the news together (follow the cooperative divorce script) or separately (follow the angry divorce script). In either case, one or both parents should be available to follow up afterward.

Children's Needs at Different Ages

When it comes to parenting, one size doesn't fit all. The same is true for talking with your children about the divorce. Each child is at a different developmental stage that will require you to adapt what you say to suit individual levels of maturity and understanding. In every developmental stage, these constants apply:

* Shield children from parental hostility and conflict.

* Give frequent reassurances of your love.

* Create and follow a predictable parenting plan.

* Remain engaged in parenting.

Infants and Young Toddlers: Birth to 18 Months

From birth to around 18 months, an infant's primary developmental task is to learn to trust and become socialized into a family. They haven't yet developed the cognitive ability to understand what a separation or divorce means. They can't use words to express what they feel, so adult caregivers must learn to observe and interpret their behavior. Signs of distress may include excessive crying, nervous or anxious behavior, fussiness, or becoming overly quiet and

How to Explain Disappearing Parents and Inappropriate Actions

People and relationships are complicated. Not all reasons for divorce can be reduced to a child-friendly explanation. Parents can find themselves trying to tackle topics like abandonment, lying, drug addiction, mental illness, alcoholism, gambling, pornography, affairs, stealing, murder, domestic violence, and sexual abuse.

Respect your children enough to give them an honest, age-appropriate explanation. Don't lie or sugarcoat it, but state the facts without blaming or putting your children in the middle. For young children, you could simply say the other parent has some grown-up problems that he must work out. For example, "Daddy has some big problems right now that he has to work on. He won't be back with us until he's better, which could be a long time."

Older children will have more familiarity with the missing parent's problems and be better able to handle a more comprehensive explanation. Name the problem, as long as it doesn't pull your children into taking sides or blaming. If you don't know where a parent is, say so. Making up an excuse to cover it up is never as helpful as you hope it will be. That said, there still may be actions that are inappropriate to discuss with even older kids. It's perfectly acceptable to set a boundary like this: "I am not willing to have this conversation with you until you are older."

nonresponsive. Infants may also show delays in achieving developmental milestones like rolling over, sitting up, crawling, walking, or talking. In addition, there could be changes in appetite, sleep patterns, or personality.

The key to helping your infant adjust to your divorce is to maintain a predictable, consistent routine. At a minimum, they need a secure, loving attachment to one adult, but it is even better to have strong attachments to both parents. Infants do best when they see each parent frequently, without going more than two or three days without seeing one parent. Give plenty of loving physical contact like rocking, holding, and nurturing play. Shield them from all arguments with their other parent.

WHAT TO DO

Infants are hardwired to pick up on your behavior. They will read your tension and the tone of your words. Pay attention to your body language when you are with the other parent, and do your best to avoid exposing your infant to stress and/or arguments.

WHAT TO SAY

When speaking to your infant around the other parent, make your tone of voice light and stress-free.

SAMPLE SCRIPT

PARENT *Time to go see Mommy!*

or

PARENT *Here you go, Daddy. Have fun!*

Older Toddlers: 18 Months to 3 Years

If you have a toddler, you are no doubt quite familiar with their strong need to be independent. They test limits and begin to express opinions. "Me do it" becomes their rallying cry. A major developmental task for toddlers is to learn to be a unique and separate individual. Temper tantrums and loudly expressed "No!"s make up what some people have termed "the terrible twos." From a developmental standpoint, there is a lot going on at this stage. It is sometimes difficult for parents to discern whether the uproar is related to the divorce or is developmentally normal. Signs of distress may include acting sad or lonely, changes in eating or sleeping habits, fears of once-familiar activities or things, and regression to behaviors from an earlier stage of development such as thumb sucking, baby talk, fear of sleeping alone, asking for a bottle, or wanting to wear a diaper again.

As with infants, providing a consistent, predictable routine where their needs are met will help your toddler adjust to the many changes divorce brings. Your toddler will need frequent reassurance of your love through your actions as well as your words. A parenting schedule where they regularly spend time with each of you is optimal. Toddlers do best going no more than three to five days without seeing one parent.

WHAT TO DO

Toddlers don't have a good concept of time so helping them know when they will be at each house will ease transition jitters. Put a calendar where they can see it and use stickers or colored pens to designate "Mom time" and "Dad time." Help them count the number of sleeps. For example, "You have three sleeps with

Mommy and then you go to Dad's house. Let's count them together. One, two, three, Daddy." The more lighthearted and matter-of-fact your tone, the better for your toddler.

Children love books about themselves. Make a small book with photographs of familiar items and routines at each parent's house and read it together before changing houses. I've known children to carry these books until the paper is nearly worn through.

Check your library or bookstore for age-appropriate books about divorce. A classic is Vicki Lansky's book *It's Not Your Fault, Koko Bear.*

WHAT TO SAY

Toddlers need a short and simple explanation about the divorce. You will likely be asked to repeat it many times as they work to understand what it means.

SAMPLE SCRIPT

PARENT   *Mommy is going to live in her house. And Daddy will live in his house. And you get to live in both places. Because we love you very much, some days you will be with Mommy and some days you will be with Daddy.*

Preschoolers: 3 to 5 Years

Preschoolers experience a huge boost in cognitive and physical abilities. They are more self-sufficient than before and able to carry out basic self-care tasks like dressing themselves, brushing their teeth, and going to the bathroom unassisted. Their vocabulary has increased, allowing them to better understand and express feelings and ideas. Preschoolers can be big talkers! Even with this growth in cognitive ability, there are still areas of confusion. For example, if they overhear parents discussing them, or arguing about parenting time, they are very likely to make the inaccurate conclusion they are responsible for the divorce.

Preschoolers benefit from routine and a predictable schedule. They can feel overwhelmed by the multiple changes that accompany divorce. They are sometimes afraid a parent will abandon them.

Preschoolers may show signs of distress like clinginess or fear of exploring the world, regressing to earlier developmental stages, feeling responsible for the divorce or a parent's feelings, acting sad, showing uncharacteristic outbursts of anger, and trying to control their environment.

WHAT TO DO

As you talk with your preschooler about the divorce, assure him of your love and abiding presence in his life. Breathe calmly, smile, and relax as you describe what's going to happen. Gently touch a hand or rub your child's back as you talk.

WHAT TO SAY

Reassurance is the name of the game with preschoolers. Tell them what's going to happen without turning it into a crisis.

SAMPLE SCRIPT

PARENT *Mom and Dad are not going to live together anymore. It makes us very sad to tell you this, but we've been having some grown-up problems that make it hard for us to get along. We'll have two houses and you will spend time with each of us. This isn't your fault. It's a problem we are having. No matter where we live, we will always be your mom and dad and take good care of you. We love you so much and that will never change.*

Early School Agers: 6 to 8 Years

School-age children are becoming quite savvy about the world. Their cognitive abilities are growing by leaps and bounds, giving them a much broader understanding of feelings and the ability to better regulate them. Family relationships are important and provide a strong base from which to venture into the world of school and friends. When the divorce disrupts this secure base, it can affect the normal developmental milestone of moving away from the family as the primary source of social interactions.

Children at this age are well aware of rules and become very disappointed when they believe a parent isn't following rules. They deeply miss the parent they are not with and sometimes side with one parent against the other.

Signs of distress include major changes in grades or attitudes about school, an increase in physical symptoms like headaches and stomachaches, exaggerated emotions like moping, crying, acting sad or lonely, and a general lack of enthusiasm.

WHAT TO DO

Provide a loving environment for your children. Maintain a predictable routine with clearly communicated expectations for behavior. Be a good listener, accepting all feelings while you help your children attach words to the feelings they share. Keep your children away from any conflict you may have with the other parent. Be that secure base they need as they go out and explore.

WHAT TO SAY

At this age, your children are going to want some details. They've probably noticed the conflict and may be anticipating your news about the divorce. Even so, they will need a gentle explanation and reassurance of your love.

MOM *You've probably noticed that your dad and I haven't been getting along very well. We've had some arguments in front of you that I'm sorry about. We've been trying to get along better, but it just isn't working, and we've decided the best thing for us is to get divorced. Do you know what that means?*

(Listen while child tells you, and then compassionately correct anything that isn't accurate)

DAD *That's right. Mom is going to stay here in this house and I am getting another house. You will get to see both of us almost every day. Some nights you'll sleep at Mom's and other nights at my house.*

MOM *We're working on a schedule right now. It's very important to us that you know this isn't your fault. Divorce is something adults do. Even with a divorce, we are still your parents and will be there for you at soccer and school and everything you do. We both love you like crazy and that will never, ever change.*

(Big hugs)

DAD *Divorce is pretty confusing to understand. Is there anything you'd like to ask us?*

Preteens: 9 to 12 Years

In this developmental stage, children are becoming even more independent, and friends take on an important role in their lives. Preteens are much more aware of what other people think, especially their peers. They might feel ashamed or embarrassed about the divorce, sometimes to the point of keeping quiet about it. They are selfishly and appropriately focused on their own lives, and they don't like it when they see the divorce messing things up for them.

Preteens have made huge leaps in cognitive ability and are much better able to understand the nuances of the problems parents are having. They are likely to feel torn between parents, and they worry when they believe a parent isn't okay. Conflicts tend to occur when they don't get something they want. They are usually very good at pushing guilt buttons, blaming parents and the divorce when things don't go as they'd like.

Signs of distress about the divorce show up in increased physical symptoms like headaches, stomachaches, or general "just not feeling well"; a dramatic change in grades or attitudes about school; fighting with peers and/or siblings; acting like the divorce is no big deal; and premature sexual activity.

WHAT TO DO

Your preteen will vigilantly watch how you handle things and will be fairly quick to judge your actions. It's important for parents to model good self-care and healthy ways to express emotions. Preteens need involved and alert parents to help them with the increasingly complex issues they face in the world. They will want to know what's going on and will push for details. Be cautious about how much you share. They can handle more information than younger children, but they still must be protected from the specifics of adult problems.

WHAT TO SAY

Your preteens will hold you accountable for your actions, sometimes brutally so. When you talk with them about the divorce, it's important to keep it real and be honest without sharing too much.

SAMPLE SCRIPT

DAD   *We want to talk with you about some changes that are going to happen in our family. After trying very hard to make our marriage work, we have decided to get a divorce. This makes us sad, but we know it's best. You've probably noticed that we are arguing quite a bit, and we can't seem to agree on much of anything. Except we do agree on two things: We love you with all our hearts and that will never change. Even though we'll be living in two houses now instead of one, we will always be your parents. We're going to make sure that you will able to do most of the things in your life that you love—like school, friends, and your favorite activities.*

MOM   *This isn't anyone's fault, especially not yours. We don't want you to think you must take sides with one of us. You love both of us. We know that. We're working out a schedule where you can spend time at each of our houses. Here's what we've been thinking about the schedule.*

(Describes the schedule)

MOM   *We'll want to hear your thoughts about how it works for you.*

DAD   *This is a lot to take in and you probably have a million feelings. So do we. It's been a very hard decision for us to make, and we want you to know we didn't make it lightly. We're here for you. Always remember that.*

Adolescents: 13 to 19 Years

The primary developmental task for adolescents is to get ready to leave home and live in the adult world. Yet they aren't quite as prepared as they may think. There are developmental milestones to achieve. They still don't have a realistic view of the future, and they lack real world experience. They have their own version of "magical thinking" where they believe bad things could never happen to them. Part of their parents' job is to compassionately help them learn responsibility for their actions as they gain experience to successfully leave the nest.

Like preteens, adolescents are focused on themselves. They resent the divorce when it disrupts their lives. Because of divorce, they may have greater responsibilities at home, less money, and overworked and unavailable parents. Cognitive ability has increased in teens to make them appear to think like adults, although they aren't quite there yet. They are really good at figuring out what's going on with their parents and will endlessly push for details. Be cautious about sharing too much because it isn't in their best interest.

Teens who are getting ready to leave home often feel anxious about this huge step and will need compassionate parents to mentally and physically be available as they work through the fear and excitement. Teens may feel some responsibility for the breakup because of things they did or did not do. It's important to reassure them the divorce in no way is their fault.

Signs of distress include premature sexual activity, excessive drug or alcohol use, problems in school including truancy or suspension, negative attitude, criticisms of parents, leaving home prematurely or showing reluctance to ever leave, canceling plans for college, and moving out.

WHAT TO DO

Maintain stability in your teen's living arrangements with as few life changes as possible. Teens need reasonable limits with clearly articulated expectations and consequences. Parents must stay attentive and keep on top of monitoring daily activities. There is great need for good communication between parents around issues like rules, curfews, homework, cell phones and Internet use, and cars.

WHAT TO SAY

Teens will be very interested in the logistics of your divorce and will do best when they have a say in the schedule. They want to know you are taking their needs into account. If possible, reassure them that their activities and interactions with friends won't change. They need to be told they aren't responsible for the divorce. Because their social lives are busy, teens do best with plenty of advance warning before changes occur in the family schedule. Offer multiple times to talk about what will happen and then compassionately answer their questions. The sample script for preteens also works for adolescents.

Finding Home Again

*W*hen she first came to see me, Tiffany was an angry sixteen-year-old. She'd gotten herself suspended from school and had moved into her nineteen-year-old boyfriend's apartment. She wasn't speaking to either of her parents, who had one of the most acrimonious divorces I'd ever witnessed. They fought about everything, but particularly about Tiffany and her younger brother Caleb. The children had become pawns in an ongoing parental tug-of-war. The parents ➡

hurled accusations about neglectful, abusive parenting back and forth, tried to recruit Tiffany and Caleb as spies, and withheld money and information about the children. They sold the family home right away. Dad moved in with his new girlfriend and Mom bought a home in a neighboring community, miles from the old neighborhood and the children's familiar schools. Tiffany and Caleb felt displaced, like refugees seeking asylum anywhere they could find it. Tiffany's grief had driven her to a dangerous place: Out of school and living with a much older boy. I worried that pregnancy would be next.

As we spoke one-on-one, Tiffany confided in me that she was sick of the games her parents continued to play. In a small, high voice, she tearfully described their family before the marriage fell apart. She longingly remembered the fun they had as a family, the summer vacations they took, and their big holiday gatherings with family and friends. Under the bravado, black eyeliner, and nose ring, I saw a terribly hurt little girl. At one of our meetings, she made this poignant observation, "I thought my job as a teenager was to grow up and leave home. But you know what? My home left me."

I cautiously began seeing Tiffany and her mother together, teaching them how to listen to each other with empathy and accept the other's feelings. I became their emotion coach, hoping to get them to talk and truly connect. It was slow going but we made progress. Next, I invited Tiffany's father to meet with her, following much the same plan. It took a very long time for them to even begin to share feelings but eventually they opened up. Tiffany agreed to meet her dad for dinner twice a month. This was tremendous progress.

About six months into our work together, Tiffany moved into her mother's house and reenrolled in school. By this time, both children were having regular parenting time with each of their parents. Most notable was that the conflict between the adults stopped. And when it did, I saw a remarkable change in Tiffany. She began smiling more and even cracked some jokes with her father at our sessions.

Privately, Tiffany asked me if I remembered when she'd said she felt that home had left her. I nodded. "Well," she said, "I think I have my home back. It's not like it used to be but it's okay." I smiled, but inside I was doing cartwheels. When parents decide to put their children first, amazing things can happen.

5

CHAPTER

Children's Reactions and Worries

You've told your children about the divorce. Now it's going to take time for reality to sink in. During your talk, your children may have seemed to understand everything you said. Chances are good they didn't—not yet. Divorce brings big changes for children, but it doesn't have to result in a negative future. In this chapter we'll cover some reactions and worries children face when parents divorce. When you know what to expect, it's much easier to provide loving guidance they can use to adapt to a new family situation.

Human beings process information with both emotion and intellect. Your children will react to the divorce with both as well. Their intellectual reaction may cause them to ask questions or dig more deeply into why the divorce is happening or perhaps who is at fault. Older children, in particular, push for answers. They are trying to make sense of something nearly impossible to understand.

Your children's worries and emotional reactions show up in their expression of feelings. They might cry with deep sadness or fear, or blow up, enraged at the news. Sometimes children sit stoically, listening but showing no feelings. These are all normal reactions and opportunities to help them understand their feelings.

Why Is This Happening to Me?

There is no doubt your children feel hurt by the divorce. It strikes at the very heart of what they've come to count on for safety and security—their family. Divorce touches every corner of a family's life so it's bound to cause big shock waves for everyone involved. Depending on their developmental stage, children will personalize the news of the divorce and wonder why it is happening to them. Don't be surprised if your child's first reaction to news of the divorce is, "But what about me? How is this going to affect my life?" Though on the surface this type of response may seem selfish or disrespectful, it's really not. It's actually a normal reaction.

During this chaotic and emotion-packed time when no one—adult or child—is at his or her best, it can be hard to hear this type of feedback from your children. My advice: Take it as an opportunity to connect deeply with your children. Use this time to help your children make sense of their feelings. Never blame or punish your children for their feelings about the divorce. Encourage your children to talk about the fears they have. What is it that worries them most? Gently and compassionately help your children understand that you are not doing this *to* them. Most importantly, reassure them as many times as they need that you will always be there for them. It will take many talks, not just the first, big one. It will be your steadfast love and presence that will comfort them as all of you adjust to this change in your family.

WHAT YOU CAN DO

- Make yourself available to talk and listen as often as your children need.

- Accept responsibility for this choice to divorce, so your children don't feel responsible.

- Help your children name their fears, worries, and the things they may feel angry about.

- Do everything you can to maintain their normal routines and lifestyle. More than anything, this will reassure them that life will go on, even in divorce.

Is This My Fault?

The hard truth is that as much as we try to protect them, children, unfortunately, carry huge burdens in a divorce. One of the most damaging of these is feeling that they are responsible for the breakup. In fact, in a survey of children who have attended her support groups, Dr. JoAnne Pedro-Carroll, an author, researcher, and therapist who works with children from divorced families, found that 79 percent worried that the family problems were their fault.

Children can mistakenly jump to the conclusion they are responsible for the divorce. Perhaps they've overheard parents arguing about their behavior, grades, or the times they fought with their siblings. When children hear their name mentioned in the context of an argument, they automatically assume they are to blame. In their childlike thinking, they believe something they did or didn't do is the reason for the divorce. Younger children will sometimes link the divorce to their actions. For example, they might tie it to having a temper tantrum or not doing something a parent asked, such as putting toys away or eating their broccoli. Consider this scenario: When told to clean up his toy cars, a young child may blurt out an angry response like, "No! You're mean. I hate you." This is usually just his lack of maturity showing. Young children don't have a wide enough vocabulary of emotions to express how they're feeling or to say something like, "I'm really having fun with my cars and I don't want to put them away just yet." If the announcement of your separation occurs close to one of these interactions, it's a very short leap for children to wrongly believe their misbehavior caused it.

Even through high school, children's cognitive abilities haven't fully developed. They tend to be concrete thinkers, seeing things with some rigidity and using a kind of black and white, either/or thinking. They also tend to be more aware of their parents' difficulties. Perhaps they've heard the arguments and felt the growing distance between Mom and Dad. But they too will still mistakenly take responsibility for the divorce. They will blame it on their bad grades, surly attitude, messy room, undesirable friends, or unwillingness to help around the house, to name just a few possibilities. And when parents argue about how to address these difficulties, it confirms for the child that he or she is the root of the problem.

- Children can quickly misinterpret what they hear, so watch what you say to others about the divorce.

- Tell your children as many times as it takes that in no way are they responsible for the divorce.

- In child-appropriate, compassionate language, explain the reasons for the divorce, being always mindful not to bad-mouth or blame the other parent.

What's Going to Happen to Me?

As we just touched on, when children hear about the divorce, a common first reaction is, "But what about me?" The two people they love more than anything in the world and who have provided for their every need will no longer be together. Children have a difficult time even imagining what that means for their lives.

Young children's fears are about their basic security. Essentially, what they want to know is, "Who will take care of me?" They wonder about details like who will prepare meals, get them to day care or school, and tuck them in at night. Their fears tend to be about practical, day-to-day caregiving and routines. Parents are children's first teachers and their main source of comfort and security. Changes to the family because of divorce bring significant losses to children.

This is an important opportunity to listen carefully to your children, and then let them know that even though you and their other parent are no longer living together, you will always be their parents. One by one, you can address their concerns. More than anything, your children need assurance that you are not abdicating your role as their parents. In later chapters we will expand upon what to say and what to do to ease your children's fears.

Older children may also worry about day-to-day caregiving, but they are much more likely to think of the divorce in terms of how it will disrupt their lives. Adults might interpret this response as selfishness, but it is more about developmentally appropriate milestones. As you've probably noticed, for older children and teens, friends are everything. For that reason, their worries tend to be much more egocentric, with questions like, "Will I still get to see my friends?" or, "What will my friends think?" They worry about being able to stay in the same school or continue with their familiar sports or other activities. They want reassurance that their lives are not going to be completely blown up.

WHAT YOU CAN DO

- Sit with children as they ask questions and tell you their concerns. Accept their anger without judgment or consequences.

- Compassionately address their specific fears.

- Give concrete information about living arrangements and parenting schedules.

- Reassure them you are not going away and will always be their parents.

What Will the Future Bring?

In divorce, children worry about the future because it is such a big unknown. What we don't know feels frightening, especially when coupled with a lack of control—the exact situation many children find themselves in. Add to that the fact that, like sponges, children soak up their parents' emotions and beliefs. If you are worried about the future—and it's completely understandable if you are—then it follows that children will feel the same. I've worked with many children who overheard their parents discussing concerns about the future that added fuel to their own already smoldering fears.

What exactly do children fear about their future? At the core, they wonder if they will be okay. It's basic survival. So much in life changes with divorce: where they live, who their friends are, if or how often they see each parent, and where they go to school or day care for starters. Plus, there are additional changes related to their sense of family identity, the amount of contact with grandparents and extended family, traditions and rituals, vacations, access to beloved pets, and perhaps a new partner in a parent's life. It's a lot to take in for anyone, especially children.

Kids sometimes hold on to hope that their parents will get back together. This so-called magical thinking means that children believe that if they want it badly enough they can make it happen. If a future reconciliation isn't likely, it's important for parents to compassionately, but firmly, say so.

Family finances can be another factor children worry about in terms of the future. In many families, divorce brings a reduction in family income. Children sometimes have big concerns about not having enough money to live on, especially if they've heard a parent voice the same concern. When they have to adjust their lifestyle to accommodate a reduced budget, children worry they won't have what they want, let alone what they need. And sometimes parents have to make tough financial decisions that affect children. Costly activities like sports, music, and special camps aren't always possible. Older children may even wonder if they'll have to change their plans about attending college.

- Listen with compassion to your children's fears.

- Help them name their worries.

- Provide age-appropriate information to address fears.

- Clear up misconceptions.

- Reassure your children that as their parents you will take care of them.

- Help children differentiate between wants and needs.

- Manage your own worry.

I Feel Invisible

Without meaning to, parents often lose sight of their children during divorce and its aftermath. They are caught in the overwhelming magnitude of details that must be addressed, while managing their own feelings of sadness, grief, fear, and anger. Their energy is focused on finding a place to live, having enough money, and surviving the process of uncoupling. If children appear to be managing well, it's one less thing to deal with in a time when there are already too many things. As one parent said to me, "It's like juggling knives. No matter what you grab hold of, it's going to hurt."

Some children have a way of sensing when their parents are on overload, and they make the choice not to add to the problem. They keep quiet about their feelings, shrugging their shoulders and uttering a nonemotional, "Okay," when parents ask how they're doing. Often, parents believe them without looking deeper because they are physically and emotionally spent. In a subtle shifting of roles, children take on the task of making their parents feel better. They become the emotional caretakers for the adults.

They take on an adult's household tasks like grocery shopping, cooking, and cleaning. On the surface this may sound like a sensitive, caring act, but it isn't what children need. Difficult as it may be during this extremely tumultuous, emotional time, it is critical that adults remain adults. Parents don't have the option of giving up their parenting tasks, no matter how helpful children may be.

Children feel invisible when they aren't told what's happening, or when they have no input into decisions about their lives. Older children complain when they are expected to follow a parenting schedule without being asked how it might work for them. In the end, parents must make the final decisions, but listening carefully to what children need and want will help them feel less invisible.

WHAT YOU CAN DO

- Request input and genuinely listen.
- Share age-appropriate details about what's happening.
- Stay in the role of parent.
- Spend frequent, quality time together.
- Deal with adult emotional issues so you're strong enough to be there for your children.

The Eight-Year-Old Adult

*A*ndrew was a bright, responsible eight-year-old. At our first meeting, I walked into the waiting room to find his mother engrossed on her phone. Andrew was scuttling across the floor, herding his two preschool age siblings away from the water cooler, where they'd been having great fun filling cups and dumping the water into the nearby wastebasket.

I could see the panic on Andrew's face. I imagine he was certain he was going to get in big trouble. I offered my warmest, friendliest smile and introduced myself. All he could manage to say was, "I'm sorry they made a mess. I'll clean it up."

I moved a bin of blocks and plastic animals in front of the preschoolers. "Don't worry about it, Andrew. I'll take care of it." His tense little body seemed to relax a bit. His mother still hadn't looked up from her phone.

Andrew was soon to meet his father, who had gone away when Andrew was an infant. They'd had no contact before this. On the surface Andrew seemed interested, maybe even excited, about meeting his dad. But he was waking up every night screaming from nightmares and he refused to go to school. His mother was worried because this behavior was out of character for her very responsible boy.

Andrew's mother worked two jobs and relied on him to take care of his brothers. She'd placed far too much responsibility on her oldest son. As I talked with Andrew, I learned that he had no friends, and though he loved to read, he didn't really like school. At home, he was responsible for doing all the laundry, keeping the house picked up, watching his brothers, making food for them, and getting them to bed. No wonder he had no friends—he had no opportunity to have them.

I worked with his mother, helping her see that Andrew was struggling under the weight of her adult expectations of him. Little by little, she reclaimed most of the parenting duties, freeing up Andrew for more age-appropriate activities such as playing ball with neighborhood friends and joining Cub Scouts.

A few weeks later I facilitated the first meeting between Andrew and his father. It went remarkably well. Andrew's dad wanted a relationship with his son, and Andrew's mother was ❯

completely supportive. We worked out a regular visitation schedule, starting slow and gradually increasing the father/son time. Eventually, Andrew's nightmares went away and he returned to school.

He still had some responsibility for his siblings, but he now also had time to be an eight-year-old boy. He and his dad rode bikes together and shared a passion for baseball. His mother confided that she was relieved to have some adult parenting help. As his parents began actively co-parenting, Andrew blossomed.

Whose Side Should I Be on . . . Mom's or Dad's?

Among the many wonderful attributes of children is their unconditional love for their parents. Your children are unendingly loyal to you, offering up their allegiance with no strings attached. Children don't play games—but, sadly, sometimes adults do.

Children can get caught in what mental health professionals call a *loyalty bind*. This is when children are caught between parents, thinking they are being disloyal to one parent if they love the other parent. When children worry about loyalty it usually is because they find themselves in the middle of parental arguments and believe they must choose one side or the other. Because your children love both of you, any expectation of one-sided loyalty creates toxic stress for them. It launches children into a tug-of-war they aren't emotionally equipped to handle. In response, they choose their words and actions with caution, trying desperately not to upset either parent.

Children get into loyalty binds in one of two ways: a parent places them there, or they place themselves there. In the first scenario, a parent causes this perhaps by hinting that they'll withdraw their love if the child doesn't take that parent's side. Here's an example: "I'm so lonely when you're with Dad. Wouldn't you rather spend Christmas with me? Besides, Dad has his new girlfriend to keep him company." This bind is clear: *I won't be okay without you, and Dad won't even notice.* Ouch!

In the second case, children place themselves in a loyalty bind with no expectation or coercion from the adults. They think it's what a parent wants, or with their childlike problem-solving skills, they decide it's the only way to reduce the pressure or make a parent happy. For example, your twelve-year-old son announces he is giving up soccer, which he loves, so he can spend more time with his dad. When you ask for more information, he tells you he doesn't think the parenting schedule is fair to his dad. "You get more time than he does and that's just not right. He's alone all the time." In this case, the child is making it his responsibility to even out the parenting schedule because he's worried about Dad.

In either scenario, the outcome for children isn't good. Children have an uncanny knack of knowing just what to say to please their parents. They learn to go for the gleam in a parent's eye, satisfied they've hit the mark, said the right thing, and pleased their parent. They breathe a sigh of relief—and wait for the next test of loyalty to arrive.

WHAT YOU CAN DO

- Genuinely encourage your children to love both of you.
- Work to manage conflict and keep your children out of the middle.

- If you see your children struggling with loyalty issues, talk about it. Help them find solutions that take them out of the tug-of-war.

- Be mindful of your words. Saying, "I'm really going to miss you," to a child could make him think he should stay with you.

Is Dad Okay?

Children are keen observers. They can accurately read body language, tone of voice, and generally understand the words their parents use. They are tuned in to emotions and sense when parents aren't doing well. That's when they worry. This is another of those big divorce burdens children can carry. They believe it's their responsibility to help their parents feel better. Mental health experts agree this reversal of roles isn't good for children. It's damaging because it places them in a no-win situation. Children have neither the skills nor experience to handle adult feelings. And yet because they love you so deeply, they will take on this gigantic task.

When your children see you crying, they want to fix whatever's bothering you. They'll do anything to make the crying stop. They notice when you are consumed by depression, unable to carry out basic day-to-day chores and activities. Some children will cover for parents by doing the best they can to keep the household running. Others worry about leaving a parent they think isn't doing well, and they feel guilty following the agreed-upon parenting schedule to spend time with their other parent.

Mood swings and emotional outbursts are terribly frightening. Children will try to compensate by retreating into the background, making no noise or demands on frazzled, unpredictable parents. They'll do anything to keep from upsetting a parent. They can do this by trying very hard to be a good child and not make waves, by avoiding mentioning the other parent or talking about things they've done at the other parent's house, or by taking over parental tasks and chores and becoming a parent's confidant. None of these is good for children because it robs them of the normal developmental tasks of simply being a child.

WHAT YOU CAN DO

- Deal with your emotions. Seek help from a licensed therapist and/or find a divorce support group.

- Talk with your children about your feelings, but reassure them that you are handling things. State clearly that it isn't their job to take care of you.

- Give your children the gift of their one and only childhood.

Mom Isn't Going to Love Me Anymore

For many families, divorce becomes an experience of scarcity, where there is never enough to go around. Money is tight and a frequent source of conflict. Children move between homes, saying good-bye to one parent as they greet the other. In some cases they lose friends, neighborhoods, family, and a comforting way of life.

All of these losses pale in comparison to the fear of losing a parent's love. Nothing is more devastating to children. A colleague of mine once said, "Children spell love: t-i-m-e." It's a powerful statement. All children benefit from having ongoing, predictable time with responsible, loving parents. It's the best way to communicate your love for them.

When a parent moves away with little preparation for children, allows gaps to occur in the parenting schedule, or misses telephone calls, or important milestones like birthdays and holidays, children fear the worst: they've lost a parent's love. Children worry that if their parents stopped loving each other, they will also stop loving them. Alleviating this fear is likely to take multiple discussions about how your love will never go away. Then your actions must support your words.

Children caught between two parents in conflict feel the stress of believing they must choose who's right and who's wrong. This loyalty tug-of-war is a losing position for children. Young children think something like this, "If I have fun with Dad, will it upset Mom? Will she be mad at me or stop loving me?"

Older children are likely to be more critical of their parents' actions, sometimes even pushing them away, when deep down what they crave is to feel loved. They want to know that their parents love them enough to accept their unacceptable behavior. One middle school client told me he worried his dad didn't love him anymore because he'd quit enforcing the rules. In response, the boy felt rudderless and unloved.

WHAT YOU CAN DO

- In words and actions, repeatedly communicate your love for your children.
- Stay actively involved as a parent.
- Spend time together.
- Follow your parenting schedule with no interruptions.
- Maintain the basic household rules and expectations that your child is used to.

Why Kids Fear Opening Up

Think about the times you've asked your children a question like, "What did you do at school today?" And they replied, "Nothing." Or you asked, "How was the party?" And their response was one word: "Fine." Sound familiar? Children are great at giving one-word, rather vague, or noncommittal answers to our questions about day-to-day life. We hear similar responses when we ask how they're handling the divorce. "Okay," they say, hoping we'll accept it and not ask again. These one-word answers are not disrespectful or an attempt to get away with an inappropriate action. It's more likely one of these reasons:

They don't have the words to express what they feel. Talking about our feelings is a skill with which many of us—adults and children—have little experience unless we've been fortunate enough to have someone teach us. Daniel Goleman, PhD, psychologist and author of the book *Emotional Intelligence*, suggests some parents are great emotion coaches for their children while others are not. When adults help children put names to what they're feeling, their emotion quotient, or EQ, rises and they improve at expressing their feelings.

They have mixed emotions. Sometimes children have two very different feelings about an experience. For example, they may be lonely for Dad and excited to spend the weekend with him. At the same time, they feel sad about leaving Mom and worry that she'll be alone. Saying hello to one parent and good-bye to the other is the reality for many children whose parents are divorced. It's hard for them to find the right label for these mixed feelings. ➡

They think you won't like or want to hear the answer. Children often try to protect a parent's feelings. They believe their answer could hurt or upset their parents, which is the last thing they want to do. Instead they choose to say as little as possible. It's another version of children trying to carry an emotional burden much too heavy for them.

They are tired or distracted. We've already talked about how important timing is when talking with children. And like adults, children get tired. A tired child isn't going to give you much. It's as simple as that. The same goes for being distracted. If you've interrupted your child in the middle of something they're enjoying, you aren't likely to have a deep, satisfying conversation. Timing *is* everything!

6

CHAPTER

Answering Your Children's Tough Questions

Your children will have questions about the divorce. That's a given. And they are likely to revisit questions at each developmental stage. Your openhearted, age-appropriate, and consistent answers will help your children repair their feelings and move forward in their lives. Younger children's questions tend to be about basic care. Older children ask more probing relationship-based questions. Either way, they will look to you for guidance and understanding as they sort through the many confusing details of life with divorce. Your words will matter.

Where's Mommy?

Fear of abandonment creates intense anxiety for children. Infants are hardwired to bond to their caregivers, and children grow and develop from that place of secure attachment. When the bond is interrupted, there are far-reaching consequences that impact healthy emotional development. For example, children may become fearful and less secure; they may believe they are responsible for the abandonment and thus unworthy of love; their feelings of self-worth and confidence are eroded; and future adult relationships are adversely affected.

As you develop your parenting plan and grapple with balancing children's needs with your own, it is crucial to be mindful of their very real fears of abandonment. You know you'd never leave them but they need to be reminded of that frequently. Children of all ages fare best with two loving and attentive parents and unencumbered access to both.

When children move back and forth between parents' homes, loss is simply part of the experience. They feel happy to be with Mom again, and at the same time, sad because they miss Dad. And vice versa. When a young child asks where a parent is, he is likely wondering at an unconscious level if he has been abandoned. Children don't have words to express these thoughts and fears. Instead they ask, "Where's Mommy?"

SAMPLE SCRIPTS

PARENT   *It sounds like you miss Mommy. Right now she's at her house. Maybe she's cooking some food or watching TV. Shall we call her so you can talk to her?*

When a parent is unavailable and you don't know how
to contact him:

PARENT *It sounds like you are thinking about Daddy. You
miss him and want to see him, but right now he's
taking a time-out and we can't call him. You could
make a picture for Daddy and we'll put it in his
special folder. Let's find your crayons.*

Who's Going to Make Dinner?

At the heart of this question is the basic inquiry, "What about me? Will
I be all right?" Young children worry about their day-to-day care. In
their childlike way, they are trying to work out who's going to do what.
It's a big task. Sometimes parents struggle with the same questions.

A frustrated and exhausted divorced parent once commented
to me that on top of everything she was handling related to the
emotional and logistical aspects of the divorce, she had to learn
to do all the things her former husband handled in the marriage.
She's right. In our busy lives, couples often divide the day-to-day
chores. When they separate, each must pick up the other's responsibilities. For example, parents who don't know how to cook must
learn at least the basics. A parent who hasn't handled the family
finances has to learn money management. And car and home
maintenance are tasks both parents must now deal with.

Children know who in their family is responsible for which tasks.
They count on the predictability and routine of it. When one parent
does something different from the way the other parent does it,
problems can arise. For example, Dad, who is new to making lunch
for the kids, cuts sandwiches in half instead of into fourths like
Mommy does. Their five-year-old is quick to point out Dad's error.
"I want Mommy's sandwiches," he may sob. What can Dad say?

DAD *You wanted me to cut your sandwich into four parts like Mommy does, right?*

(Child nods)

DAD *It surprised you when you saw only two halves, and you didn't like it.*

(Child nods again)

DAD *That's easy to fix. Now that I know what you like, I can do it your way.*

Why Don't You Love Daddy Anymore?

Understanding love and why it ebbs and flows is complex to say the least. Countless experts have devoted careers to studying the topic, and yet many of us are still mystified when it comes to relationships. It's even more confusing for children. They have no understanding of the nuances adults feel. It's black or white. Either you love someone or you don't. And, to kids, not loving a family member anymore is unimaginable.

As adults, we do our best to explain that adult love is different from the love parents have for their children. We emphasize that parents never stop loving their children. But honestly, it's tricky. When parents abandon children or abuse them, these destructive actions further complicate how children view love.

If your child puts you on the hot seat and wants to know why you no longer love the other parent, take a deep breath. Give yourself time to think. Don't blurt out the first thing that comes to mind because it likely won't be your best answer. Tailor your reply to your child's age and cognitive ability.

These guidelines will help:

- Reassure your children that you will never stop loving them. There is *nothing* they could do that would cause you not to love them.

- Reiterate that adult love is completely different than the love parents have for their children.

- Be honest without sharing inappropriate or excessive details.

- Be concrete not vague. For example, "We are arguing a lot," or, "We don't want to be with each other," instead of, "Our values are different."

- Acknowledge how confusing and unsettling this is for children.

- Never speak negatively about the other parent.

- If appropriate, describe positive feelings other than love that you have for the other parent. For example, "Your mom is a hard worker and I admire her for that." Or, "Your dad takes such good care of you. I really respect him for that."

SAMPLE SCRIPT

PARENT *Love can be kind of confusing. Parents love children no matter what happens, and it's permanent. Nothing you do will make our love for you go away. But love between grown-ups sometimes does change. And when it does, it's no longer comfortable to stay together. Your dad gave me you, and I will always be grateful to him. And we will be your parents forever, just not together.*

Will You and Mom Get Back Together?

Children of all ages fantasize that their parents will reconcile. Even into their late teens and early twenties, when asked if they could change anything about the divorce, they will reply, "I wish my parents were back together." Children hold fast to this tiny thread of hope despite knowing deep in their hearts it will never happen. They are usually painfully aware of the reasons reconciliation won't work, and yet still they dream.

Your children deserve an honest answer. With this question there is no room for anything but a yes or no answer. If you don't have one, then it is not the right time to tell your children about the divorce. If you know without a doubt that you are not getting back together, you must say so, gently and with compassion. Don't lead them on or suggest that *maybe* you'll reconcile. And please, don't tell your children the decision rests with the other parent. Never say, "I want to get back together but your dad doesn't. I'm hoping he'll change his mind." This is a terrible burden for your children and amounts to emotional blackmail. Also, don't encourage children to think they can get you back together, no matter what books and movies might suggest. Your best move: Remind your children that the divorce is an adult decision and there's nothing they can do to get their parents back together. As always, reassure them of your love and commitment to them.

SAMPLE SCRIPTS

For young children:

PARENT *I know you miss Mommy and wish we were all living in the same house like we used to. But sweetie, that isn't going to happen. We've made our decision.*

Mommy has her house now, and I have mine. And you have two houses. We love you so much and will take care of you no matter where we live. We are your parents and that will never, ever change.

For older children:

PARENT   *We know this divorce isn't something you want, and we're really sorry it's so hard on you. It wasn't an easy choice for us to make. We tried hard to fix our marriage, but we couldn't. We're getting a divorce, and that won't change, but we do promise to make your life run as smoothly as we can. We love you and will never put you in the middle. We are still your parents and will be always.*

French Braids and PB&Js

*E*ric is a divorced father of twin eight-year-old daughters. When he and his wife separated, he knew almost nothing about his girls. He was a web designer who spent most of his waking hours in front of the computer. His work schedule was a big contributor to the demise of his marriage.

He laughed when he recalled for me his first week of parenting time with the girls two years earlier. "It was a disaster," he said. "I didn't have a clue about what they needed, and their mom wasn't about to tell me. I think she hoped I'd fail, and I nearly did. I tried to force them into my lifestyle and my routines, but they didn't want that." Eric went on to describe how the girls weren't interested in watching ❯

bicycle racing on television with him. They wanted to have tea parties and play with their dolls. And they wanted nothing to do with their dad's Paleo diet. They liked cereal for breakfast and peanut butter and jelly sandwiches for lunch.

After the disastrous first week, the girls balked at returning to their dad's house. Eric was devastated. "I was really hurt when they didn't want to see me," he said. "Something just snapped in me and shook me out of my selfish ways. I knew I needed to learn how to be a good dad. I wanted that more than anything."

Eric enrolled in several local parenting classes and began to learn how to relate better to his daughters. He made food they liked and got quite good at sharing tea and make-believe cookies with their stuffed animals. His daughters responded to his efforts by eagerly coming to his house on his parenting days. His ex-wife noticed his new focus on their daughters and began to share parenting information with him.

About six months later, Eric walked into my office beaming. He pulled out a certificate of completion and held it up for me to read. It was from a class on French braiding hair. He said it was the most fun he'd had in a long time. "I was the only man there, but it didn't matter. I think I'm a natural at it," he said with a smile. Then he showed me photos of his two girls, each sporting beautiful French braids. "I knew if they were ever going to want to spend the night at my house, I had to learn how to do their hair."

Eric saw firsthand the huge pay-off for everyone involved when a parent learns to put his children's needs first.

What Do I Tell My Friends?

As children get older, peer pressure and their friends' opinions become very important. Fitting in is the driving force in most children's lives from about the age of six through high school (and occasionally beyond). The last thing kids want is to be different.

In general, children don't often share the details of what's happening in their families. Except for very close friends who may spend time in each other's homes, many children have no idea that a classmate's parents are divorced. They simply don't talk about it. However, if parents argue with each other at school, or otherwise create a scene, children are terribly embarrassed. Emotionally responsive parents understand this and do their level best to create a conflict-free zone around their children.

The need to fit in is particularly stronger for adolescents. Their peer group is everything to them. As the divorce becomes a reality, teens are likely to seek comfort with their friends. It doesn't mean they are talking about what's going on. They probably aren't. More likely they find solace just hanging out together. Savvy parents recognize how important peers can be, especially at this emotionally difficult time.

Divorce may require children to move away from friends—to a different neighborhood and school or an entirely new town. This is another significant loss following the losses that already accompany the divorce. Sometimes emotionally exhausted parents are unable to appreciate the depth of these losses and minimize their children's reactions. Be mindful of how important your children's friends are to them as you talk them through this tough time.

PARENT *When something big like divorce happens in your family, it's hard to face your friends. You might wonder if they think it's your fault, or that your family is totally messed up. But here's the thing to remember: All families go through hard times. Right now, ours is. But we'll get through this. The divorce is about Mom and Dad, not your friends. You can spend time with them like always. That won't change.*

If the new living arrangements means your child must move away from friends:

PARENT *It's really hard to move away from your friends. They're important to you. It must make you feel angry. You've already had so many changes with our divorce. This doesn't feel fair. Right now we don't have a choice about moving, but you do have a choice about staying in touch with your friends. We can arrange times to get together. You can call or text them. It may take a bit of planning, but you don't have to lose touch with your friends.*

Why Are You Crying?

Adults sometimes feel uncomfortable or believe they shouldn't allow children to witness their emotions. Nothing could be further from the truth. Children learn to understand, express, and regulate their own feelings based on what they observe their parents doing. Parents who understand their important role as emotion coaches for their children welcome every opportunity to teach children about feelings.

Divorce is an experience that brings up intense emotions for adults and children. It's an ongoing process that unfolds over time rather than as one single event. At each stage, feelings emerge. When parents try to dismiss their feelings, never showing sadness or grief about the end of the marriage, children may be led to believe the marriage held little meaning in the first place. It becomes one of the first painful lessons children receive about not being able to trust love. It also sends a strong message to children that they must hide or dismiss their feelings too. On the other hand, when parents cry or otherwise show their feelings about the divorce, it models for children that expressing feelings is normal and acceptable behavior. Grieving what has been lost through divorce is an important step in healing.

Older children and teens may have what appears to be a more cynical reason for asking you why you're crying. In their more rigid style of thinking, they will hold you accountable for your actions with comments like, "If you wanted the divorce, then you shouldn't be crying about it." Ouch. Their own pain is being expressed as shame, blame, and judgment. Rather than responding defensively, make it an opportunity to listen with empathy. By listening without returning the judgment, you can help your children name and explore their feelings. It becomes a powerful opportunity for closeness.

SAMPLE SCRIPTS

For young children:

PARENT *I'm crying because I feel very sad about getting divorced. Even though it's the right choice for us, there are many things I'll miss about our family. Your dad and I had some really good times together before our marriage stopped working for us. Remembering those makes me sad.*

PARENT   *I'm crying because I'm feeling sad. Our decision to get divorced is probably the hardest choice I've ever made. Mom and I tried really hard to fix the things in our marriage that weren't working, but in the end we just couldn't. That makes me sad. I know this is hard on you, which is something I never intended, and I'm sorry for that.*

For teens:

PARENT   *You're right, your dad and I did want the divorce. It's the best decision for us, even though it was very hard to make. Feelings are rarely all or nothing. I still feel sad about all the changes this divorce will bring to our family. I'll miss the things we did together. But I also feel relieved to be away from the tension and the arguments.*

Is Dad Coming to My Birthday Party?

As you go through the first year of your divorce, you must work out how to celebrate family traditions, holidays, and birthdays. As each family situation is unique, there isn't one right way to handle holidays and celebrations. Some divorced parents continue to celebrate special occasions together, while others keep everything separate. There are several things to consider as you decide what's best for your family.

First, look honestly at your comfort level at being in the same room with the other parent. If you are miserable and barely holding yourself together, it won't be a good experience for you or your

Talking about Domestic Violence

Parents are responsible for their children's safety. In the best of all worlds, this would never be an issue. Unfortunately, every day, children are exposed to family violence. The National Child Traumatic Stress Network offers this definition of domestic violence: "A pattern of behavior that one person in a relationship uses to control the other. The behavior may be verbally, emotionally, physically, financially, or sexually abusive."

When children are abused or know abuse is happening in their family, they are overwhelmed with feelings and questions. A caring parent is the best resource for children to answer questions and provide support and safety. Parents may also enlist the help of a mental health professional.

If there is a restraining order in place against one parent, keep your explanation to children simple and don't assign blame. For example, you can say, "Right now, Dad is having a problem managing his anger. While he works on getting better, you're going to take a break from spending time with him."

As you talk with your children, emphasize these points:

- Violence in the family is never the child's fault.
- My job as your parent is to keep you safe.
- Hurting people is never okay.
- You don't have to keep secrets.
- Fixing family problems isn't your job. You don't have to take care of me.
- I'm here for you, to love you, to listen to you, and to answer your questions.

children. They'll read your stress and probably "catch" it. If there is any chance of conflict, avoid joint celebrations. Two separate, stress-free holidays are much better than one that's filled with tension or conflict. I've found that children are actually thrilled with two birthday parties or holiday celebrations.

Second, be sure that getting together as a family for holidays doesn't give your children mixed signals. You don't want to add fuel to a reconciliation fantasy they may be harboring. The same goes for adults. If you secretly hope attending family holidays will spur reconciliation between you and your former spouse, you're missing the point. These celebrations are for your children.

Third, determine what is truly good for your children. What do they want? How will they be able to enjoy the day? Are you encouraging a joint celebration out of guilt or with your children's best interests in mind?

When a child asks you if the other parent will attend a special celebration, your answer will vary depending on the circumstances. Use these general guidelines as you prepare your reply.

BE HONEST

If you know the other parent isn't planning to attend, say so. It is disappointing and deeply painful for a child when he or she expects to see a parent who is a no-show. That experience will color their memory of the celebration or holiday.

AGREE TO A CONFLICT-FREE ZONE

Give your children the gift of no conflict in their presence. Think how awful it would be to remember Thanksgiving as the time Mom and Dad got in a big fight. No conflict *ever* would be an even greater gift.

WORK OUT AND FOLLOW A PLAN

Whether you agree to alternate holidays, have two separate events, or attend one together, keep your word. Be a reliable parent your children can count on.

KEEP NEGATIVE FEELINGS TO YOURSELF

Even though the plan you develop may not be your first choice, don't tell your children. Make the best of the day and remember you are doing it for them.

GET CREATIVE

After divorce, holidays and family occasions can bring up many painful feelings. Trying to recreate the old celebrations often exaggerates the grief that is a normal part of divorce. Instead, create new celebrations and traditions. For example, take a family hike on Thanksgiving, organize an outdoor picnic for a summer birthday, or volunteer for a community event. Get your children involved in the plans.

Why Are You Fighting?

"When elephants fight, it is the grass that suffers." This saying from the Kikuyu tribe in Kenya beautifully expresses what happens to children when parents fight. They suffer.

Parental conflict is frightening and leaves children feeling overwhelmed, helpless, and abandoned. They have no way to understand why the two people they love most in the world can't get along. Adults argue over huge issues like resources, parenting time, child welfare, and responsible actions. They also argue over hurt feelings, sadness, shame, embarrassment, and fear.

Anger is simply an emotion; it is a warning signal letting us know things aren't quite right. When adults are able to disagree and resolve issues, it models a healthy way of problem solving for children. If children overhear an argument, follow up with them to make sure they aren't frightened or misunderstanding what happened. It's also important to let them know that an issue is resolved. Disagreements are part of family life, and children need to learn how to solve and resolve them.

The danger for children lies in being exposed to escalating, out-of-control, over-the-top conflict between their parents. It's the biggest predictor of poor outcomes for children on a wide variety of measures including school performance, physical health, mental health, and future adult relationships. If you have a limited amount of energy to deal with things after divorce, learning to manage anger is the place to start.

If your child overhears an argument and wants to know why you're fighting, include these in your explanation:

- Reassure your child that she isn't responsible for the fight.

- Apologize for your angry words or out-of-control behavior.

- Listen with empathy and acknowledge his feelings.

- Reassure her of your love.

- Let your child know when you've solved the problem.

SAMPLE SCRIPT

DAD   *I'm sorry you heard me fighting with Mom. I was upset and said some unkind things to her.*

CHILD   I don't like it when you fight.

DAD *It must be scary when Mom and I get into arguments.*

CHILD *(Nods head)* I'm afraid you might hurt each other.

DAD *You worry our arguments will turn into a physical fight?*

CHILD Uh-huh.

DAD *I promise you that will never happen. I'm so sorry you are carrying around that big worry.*

CHILD You should take a time-out if you think you're going to fight with each other.

DAD *(Smiles) That's what we ask you to do, isn't it?*

CHILD You tell me to go to my room and calm down.

DAD *Well it's good advice that Mom and I will follow too. We don't want to scare you. We love you too much to upset you.*

7

CHAPTER

Responding to Sticky Situations

Even in the best co-parenting situations problems can still arise. Feelings change, miscommunication occurs, or children present new challenges. Just when you think you've got everything figured out, and are maybe even patting yourself on the back, well . . . you know what happens next. Fortunately, these course changes are opportunities to connect more deeply with your children and to model valuable life skills. In this chapter, we'll talk about tricky situations you might face and the best way to handle them.

Taking Sides

Sometimes, more than anything, we want our children to side with us in the divorce. We want to feel that our actions are justified, to soothe our grief or guilt, and to feel less alone. This is a normal feeling, and yet it's unhealthy for our children. We may try to convince ourselves we *are* doing the right thing. We *are* putting our children first. But if we want them to take sides, we've stepped off the path.

Conventional divorce advice is clear: Keep children out of the middle, don't expose them to adult conflict, and never bad-mouth the other parent. This is the very advice I give the families with whom I work. It's sound advice but, admittedly, not always easy to follow. Your relationship with your former spouse may be strained, and you may feel angry, hurt, betrayed, or disappointed. Frankly, there are times you'd like never to see the other parent again.

Criticizing Mom or Dad

When your child makes a negative comment about the other parent, secretly you may be pleased. Your hurt feelings and bad experiences are validated, and it feels good. The problem: This isn't helpful for children. Once again, it draws them into the dangerous territory of feeling conflicted about their loyalty to you versus their loyalty to their other parent. How you choose to respond to your child's negative comment makes a big difference. Your response can either downplay the comment, and keep your child out of the middle of your conflict, or it can escalate the situation.

Years ago I was browsing in a gift shop and saw a plaque that read, "The best gift a father can give his children is to love their mother." If we adapt the sentiment slightly it works for divorce. "The best gift divorced parents can give their children is respect for each other as parents." With those words of wisdom in mind, it's easier to know what to do and say when your child speaks badly about the other parent. Also, remind your child that there are times in even the healthiest of families that we get upset with each other. We may yell, act badly, or say something unkind. It doesn't mean we want to leave the family. All feelings, negative and positive, are opportunities to improve our ability to communicate and better understand our feelings.

WHAT TO DO

- Acknowledge your child's feelings
- Listen with empathy
- Remain neutral and set appropriate boundaries

WHAT TO SAY

Make it clear that you're not asking your child to side with you. Avoid adding your own opinions or grievances about the other parent.

SAMPLE SCRIPT

PARENT   *It sounds like you're really upset with your dad. I want you to know that you don't have to share my feelings about Dad. In fact, that's the last thing I want. He is your only father and it's super important for him to be part of your life. Talk to him and tell him what's bothering you.*

Repeating Trash Talk

Your children may come to you after spending time with the other parent and repeat negative comments that were said about you. The natural reaction is to feel defensive and hurt and to lash out with negative comments of your own. Natural? Yes. Emotionally healthy?

No. As you've learned throughout this book, divorce done well asks a lot of adults, and this is one of those times. Rather than lashing out, apply your child filter: What response is best for my children?

The answer is to keep a cool head and not react. No drama, please. Stay in your role as a parent. Watch your body language to make sure it supports comments you can make such as:

- Hmm. (Yep, that's it!)
- Your mom and I see things differently.
- If you have questions for me, just ask. I'm happy to talk with you.
- It's not your job to tell me what Dad says. I'll talk directly with him.

Two Homes, Two Sets of Rules

Each parent will have different house rules in their post-divorce homes. This takes adjustment for children as they move back and forth between parents. Fortunately, children are adept at adjusting to differing rules for each home and are typically more flexible than adults in this way. They quickly learn, for example, that rules at daycare or school differ from those at home, and they adapt. They are able to apply this experience to Mom's rules versus Dad's rules with minimal difficulty.

Harder for adults is the often-disconcerting realization that they have no power over what happens at the other parent's house. The rules for bedtime, chores, curfew, discipline, and family routines frequently vary from home to home. Successful co-parents come to accept that unless a situation has to do directly with them, or is about their child's immediate health or welfare, what happens at the other parent's home isn't their business. That said, it always helps children when both parents have similar rules and expectations. If parents can agree on a basic set of behavioral guidelines, there will be less confusion and potential conflict.

Children will sometimes try to manipulate their parents to get what they want. Does this statement sound familiar? "Why do I have to go to bed at 8:30? Mom lets me stay up until 10." The parent who receives this message has a choice. He can take the bait and possibly get into an argument or issue an ultimatum. For example, "I don't care what your mom says. She was always too easy on you. Go to bed at 8:30 or you lose your television privileges for the weekend."

The other option is to offer a more thoughtful reply. "It must be confusing to have two different bedtimes. I can't say what happens at Mom's house because that's between you and her. But at my house, you have all my time and attention until your bedtime at 8:30. Then afterward I need time to get things done. Can you live with that?"

With household rules, keep these in mind:

- Two houses usually mean two sets of rules.

- You don't have influence over the other parent's house.

- It isn't realistic to expect the other parent to apply your disciplinary action at his/her home. For example, he grounds your son and then expects you to also ground him. Separate houses, separate consequences.

- Always respect the other parent's rules and ask your children to do the same.

Counseling for Kids

It might surprise you to know that when parents separate and/or divorce, most children don't need counseling, especially right away. The key factor is how their parents choose to behave. In his book, *The Truth about Children and Divorce*, Robert Emery, PhD, states, "Good parenting is good therapy." What he means by this is that children are more likely to adjust well to the divorce when their parents recognize their needs and make good parenting choices to address them. For children to make their way through their parents' divorce unscathed, they need these seven important things:

1. Parents who remain actively engaged
2. Low to no drama or ongoing conflict
3. Access to both parents and two loving homes
4. No denigration of the other parent
5. Emotionally responsive parents who listen and accept all feelings
6. Predictable routines and schedules
7. "Normal" lives

This list may seem daunting, especially in the midst of the craziness of divorce. And yet it is a basic formula for success.

If parents are unable to provide one or more of these seven things, a mental health professional may be able to help. Counseling gives children a safe place to work through their feelings and feel validated as they try to make sense of what's going on in their family. A skilled therapist is sometimes better suited than a parent to coach children through the ups and downs of the divorce. Depending on the issues and their intensity, a child ○

may see a counselor alone; other times a parent and child will go together. There may even be times when the entire family meets with the counselor. The goal always is to help children adjust to the many changes in their lives that come with their parents' divorce.

If you are seeking a mental health professional for your child, look for someone who is licensed in their field, has at least a few years of experience, and specializes in issues related to separation and divorce. Therapists should readily answer your questions about their credentials and experience.

In divorces where there are disputes over custody and parenting time, children may see a mental health professional as part of a court-ordered evaluation. There are many extremely well-qualified, compassionate professionals who do this work. But even so, it is usually uncomfortable and even frightening for children. The idea of having a stranger make decisions about their family is a difficult concept to grasp. Unless they are very young, children know exactly what's going on between their parents. It places them squarely in the middle of their parents' conflict. In some cases, parents share far too much with their children, which only adds to their discomfort and awkwardness.

It's time to call in a qualified mental health professional if your child shows any of the following signs:

- Talk about self-harming or suicide
- Dramatic change in behavior
- Victim of domestic violence or sexual abuse
- Ongoing behavior that is out of control
- Harming pets
- Eating disorders
- Refusal to attend school or problems at school
- Violent behavior
- Prolonged depression
- Substance abuse
- Premature sexual behavior

Understanding Resistance

When we ask children to live their lives traveling back and forth between parents, we often don't realize how truly complicated it is for them. To everyone's credit, the great majority of children in divorced families manage this with relative ease. However, problems do arise. Occasionally a child will stage a rebellion and boldly announce he no longer wants to go to Mom's or Dad's. Sadly, some parents use this as an excuse to create or continue conflict by blaming each other or initiating court action. They assume the worst about each other, suggesting the child doesn't want to go because the other parent is doing something wrong. Of course, keeping children safe is every parent's first obligation and safety concerns must be explored. More often, the reason has nothing to do with abuse or neglect.

Perhaps what your child wants is simply to have a voice. When parents put their children's needs first, they begin by listening with empathy to understand what's going on. They don't point fingers or blame the other parent. Instead they bring an attitude of curiosity to their conversations with their child. The reason for not wanting to go to the other parent's house could be any number of things, including not having a room or space of their own, feeling home-sick in a new place, worrying about the parent left behind, missing friends or activities, feeling lonely or bored, not having their things, unhappy with the rules/expectations or a parent's new relationship, or simply needing a break from going back and forth.

Once parents understand and children feel heard, they can begin to create solutions. This is another excellent opportunity to model healthy emotional behavior. Use these messages to help your children feel heard:

- "I want to know how you feel."
- "I'm here to listen."
- "All feelings are okay."
- "I won't punish you for your feelings."
- "We can find a good solution."

It's important to let children know through your words and actions that you value their relationship with the other parent and want them to spend time together. Children can get caught between parents, feeling disloyal to one if they spend time with the other. The more you are able to keep your child out of this emotionally dangerous loyalty conflict, the better.

SAMPLE SCRIPT

When your child doesn't want to spend time with the other parent:

DAD   *It seems like you've changed your mind about spending time at Mom's.*

CHILD   Yeah. I don't want to go there anymore.

DAD   *That's a big change.*

CHILD   I know.

DAD   *Your face looks a little sad.*

CHILD   Uh-huh.

DAD   *Is there something that makes you sad about going to Mom's?*

CHILD   She'll be sad if I don't want to go.

DAD   *Mmm. You're worried about making Mom sad?*

CHILD   She's sad all the time. She cries a lot.

DAD   *So when you're at Mom's she cries?*

CHILD   Uh-huh. It's not very fun.

DAD   *I see. When Mom is crying it's no fun for you.*

CHILD   Yeah. I just stay in my room, but there's nothing to do.

DAD   *You wish you had some of your things at Mom's.*

CHILD   Could I take my iPad when I go?

DAD   *You think if you had your iPad it would help?*

CHILD   *(Nods)*

DAD   *I'll need to check with Mom first.*

CHILD   Okay, let's ask her now.

This conversation doesn't completely solve the problem, but it offers a start. The child feels heard and not judged. If the parents are able to work together as co-parents, they can collaborate to find a solution—perhaps involving the iPad, perhaps not.

When a child doesn't want to come to your house, it hurts. The natural reaction is to take it personally. "She doesn't love me anymore," you think, or you feel the other parent put the child up to it. Chances are, neither of these thoughts is true. It is more likely one of the reasons suggested above. Don't pressure your child into wanting to come to your house or make her feel guilty. Listen with empathy and then generate a solution together.

When your child doesn't want to come to your house:

MOM	*Sounds like you want a break from coming to my house.*
CHILD	Sort of.

MOM	*It's kind of hard to tell me.*
CHILD	Yeah. I don't want to make you mad.

MOM	*You're worried I'll be mad.*
CHILD	Uh-huh.

MOM	*That can't feel very good.*
CHILD	No. I don't want you to be mad or sad.

MOM	*Going back and forth is hard.*
CHILD	Yeah. I don't want overnights anymore.

MOM	*Spending the night at two houses is tiring.*
CHILD	Uh-huh.

MOM	*What if you come to my house on our regular days, and I take you back to Dad's to sleep?*
CHILD	*(Face relaxing)* So we could still see each other?

MOM	*Yes. Would that help?*
CHILD	Uh-huh. You could help me with homework?

MOM	*You bet.*

Issues with Affection

There will be times when your child squirms away from a hug or refuses to say she loves you. This is normal developmental behavior and usually has little to do with the divorce. It's more likely a bid for independence. To help our children become emotionally healthy, we must give them choices about their bodies, and then respect their requests. Never force affection on a child or demand robot-like utterances. An "I love you" is only meaningful when it's an authentic expression of a feeling. If you ask for a kiss and receive a no, accept it with grace. The same goes for other forms of physical contact. Let your child take the lead. If he's comfortable climbing on you, initiating holding hands, or roughhousing, then a spontaneous hug may be perfectly appropriate. But if he shies away, stop immediately and respect the boundary he's set.

Likewise, don't tell children to hug or kiss the other parent. Allow them to set the pace. Sometimes a parent will ask, "Do you have a hug for me?" This is a respectful request, but you have to be willing to accept the no if it comes. Teaching children that they have control over their bodies will help them become skilled at setting those very important boundaries they'll need as teens and young adults. Learning that "no means no" starts early.

Troublesome Transitions

Going back and forth between parents is tough on children and can be a prime time for meltdowns. Put yourself in your child's shoes. What would it be like to essentially live out of a backpack? Invariably there'll be times that the thing you want or need—your favorite sweatshirt or the book you're halfway through—is at the other house. Now add in two sets of rules and perhaps a different cast of characters in each house and top it off with a dash of tension between parents. It's a recipe for disaster that millions of families live every single day. And all things considered, most kids handle it pretty well.

Sometimes however, children falter under the pressure. You may notice temper tantrums, regression to earlier developmental stages, clinginess, manipulative behavior, and fighting with siblings. Increased anger, changes in school behavior, isolation from friends, physical symptoms, anxiety, and depression are all signs that children are struggling.

Use these suggestions to guide your children through the stress of transitions:

CREATE AND FOLLOW PREDICTABLE TRANSITION ROUTINES

For example, on your first night together always cuddle on the couch and watch a movie. Or perhaps take a bike ride or make dinner together. Keep transition days low-key so you have plenty of opportunity to reconnect.

UPDATE THEM ON YOUR LIFE

Share what's been going since they last were with you. For example, "While you were at Dad's, Cooper broke out of the yard three times and I had to go find him."

KEEP INTERACTIONS WITH THE OTHER PARENT CORDIAL

Do your best to ensure that the transitions are drama-free. You may not be able to influence the other parent, but you are 100 percent in charge of your actions. Behave in a businesslike manner—no arguments and no bad-mouthing. Handle parenting business another time, away from your children.

GIVE YOUR CHILDREN SPACE

They may need time to settle back into your household, into their rooms, and to reacclimate to the routines and expectations of your home. Don't take it personally if a child needs some alone time to decompress.

SPEND TIME WITHOUT NEW PARTNERS

Your children want to be with you, not your new love interest. When your kids have just returned from the other parent's house isn't the time to get everyone together. Introduce new partners slowly. We'll talk about this in depth in the next chapter, but for now keep this rule of thumb in mind: At the beginning of a new relationship, follow the 80/20 rule. Eighty percent of the time you should be with your children alone. Twenty percent of the time you can include your new partner.

PROVIDE YOUR CHILDREN WITH WHAT THEY NEED TO BE COMFORTABLE

When possible, keep important items at both homes. If your child realizes he's forgotten something at the other parent's home, help him retrieve it without a fuss.

DON'T MAKE YOUR CHILD A MESSENGER

If you have something to say to the other parent, do it yourself. Never put your children in the role of courier. Something you consider a simple request can escalate into an uncomfortable situation. Consider your children's feelings and keep them out of the middle.

8

CHAPTER

Looking Forward

As you move through the process of divorcing and then parenting apart, you will find that many of the problems you faced early on will resolve and life will settle into a comfortable routine for you and your children. And just when you think it's finally smooth sailing, you or the other parent will move or fall in love, and life will get challenging again. Here are some strategies to keep you moving in a positive direction.

Staying Connected

To thrive, your children need ongoing, concrete, observable demonstrations of your love. This is easier when you live in the same town and are able to spend regular time together. However, it's certainly still doable when you live a distance from your children. It just takes more planning and creativity to maintain the bond. Staying connected is one of the most important things you'll do for and with your children. It's not always easy. They may not always be available when you call, for instance, or when you do connect with them, they may have little to say to you. It is still very much worth your effort. Believe me, your children will notice.

The older your children are, the more complicated it is for them to find time for you. Hard as this is on parents, it's normal for tweens and teens to focus on their peers and social activities instead of their parents. When you live in the same town or less than an hour or two drive away, your primary means of connecting with your children when they aren't with you revolves around their lives and schedules. This can mean attending school and social events and extracurricular activities, meeting for a meal, treating for the occasional ice cream run, or keeping in touch with phone calls and texts. When you live far away from your children, the responsibility to stay connected falls to you, not them. It takes persistence, creativity, and a good dose of humility. Here are a few things to know about different means of keeping in contact.

PHONE CALLS

Most parenting plans include a plan for telephone calls. While they are one of the common ways for parents and kids to stay in touch, I've found that they can be frustrating for many families. Here's why: A parent will call at the designated time only to find that their child is unavailable or distracted and not interested in talking. Try not to take it personally, and don't let a less-than-enthusiastic reception deter you from phoning. Even a quick call to say, "I love you. Hope you had an awesome day," is enough to let your child know you're thinking of her.

TEXTING

Many parents and grandparents learn to text just so they can communicate with the children in their lives. These days, texting is a more child-approved mode of communication than email or phone calls. Shoot quick texts to say, "Hey, I'm thinking about you," or, "How was your piano lesson?" or send a photo you know your child will enjoy. Get creative and silly with your notes and keep your texts light. Never use texting to criticize or discipline. The point is to enjoy the connection, so save the serious stuff for your next face-to-face or phone call.

VIDEO CHATS

Skype and FaceTime are two of the most popular visual communication tools and are wonderful ways for parents to have a conversation, read a bedtime story, give a tour of their home, or simply see their children. For young children, video chatting requires the other parent's cooperation, which hopefully is never a problem.

MAIL

Children love finding surprises in the mail so don't underestimate the power of receiving a letter, card, or package the "old-fashioned" way. A thoughtful card, a fun postcard, or a small gift with a note saying, "I saw this and thought of you" are simple, sweet ways to let your child know she's on your mind even when you're not together.

Warming Up to New Relationships

Chances are it's going to happen at some point. You and/or your former spouse will enter into a new relationship. Right now, romance and dating may be the last things on your mind, but as time goes on you will probably find yourself ready to get involved with someone else. After all, at our cores we human beings are hardwired to be paired. The real challenge is not so much about the "if or when" of a new relationship, but "how." We'll discuss how you can make it smooth and as low-stress as possible for everyone involved.

Relationships after divorce are usually more complicated than the first time around. You and your children are now a package deal. Before you were free to simply follow your own feelings and desires, but now you must also consider the needs and well-being of your children. The prevailing wisdom is to take it slowly. In the beginning, keep your dating life private. Children are rarely enthusiastic about a parent's new partner so don't involve your kids until you know the relationship has some staying power. And even then, always be sure to spend some alone time with your children. Remember the 80/20 rule we talked about in chapter 7. At least in the beginning, give your children solo time with you about 80 percent of the time. Similarly, don't force a "new family" on them too soon or expect that they'll be pleased about it. A new relationship will take time, a great deal of talking and listening, and sensitivity to get your children onboard.

When the Other Parent Has a New Relationship

Hearts are vulnerable following divorce. Even though the divorce may have been a joint decision, initiated by you, or something you've come to accept, it's often painful to hear that your former spouse is in a new relationship. It's normal for a variety of emotions to surface, including jealousy, anger, grief, and fear to name some big ones. It helps to know ahead of time when a new person will be introduced into your child's life. It's an aspect of respectful co-parenting that will help children adjust. But what if you haven't had a heads-up about a new relationship, and your child announces that Dad has a new girlfriend? How do you handle it? What if your child then says, "I hate her. She's mean to me"?

First, sidestep your jealousy or other feelings and focus on your child. Listen with empathy to find out what he's thinking and feeling. Here's a sample of some thoughtful dialogue:

SAMPLE SCRIPT

MOM   *It sounds like you're not happy about Dad's girlfriend.*
CHILD Why does he have to have a girlfriend anyway?

MOM   *You wish we were still a family?*
CHILD Uh-huh. She's not like you.

MOM   *Dad's house feels different when she's there.*
CHILD Yeah. She made eggs for breakfast.

MOM   *(Smiles) You don't like eggs at all.*
CHILD Nope.

MOM	*Getting used to Dad having a girlfriend is hard.*
CHILD	I wish she wasn't around.

MOM	*It seems like Dad likes her.*
CHILD	I know. I saw them kissing.

MOM	*Hmm.*
CHILD	Is she going to be my new mom?

MOM	*No. I'm your mom and always will be. But she could be a friend.*
CHILD	(Thinking)

MOM	*It might help to tell your dad how you're feeling.*
CHILD	I guess.

This conversation doesn't solve the problem, but it opens the door to the discussion. There's no judgment or conflict from the parent to overpower the child's feelings.

The next step is to follow up in a businesslike way with the other parent. Child safety is always the first thing to ensure. Your child telling you "she's mean to me" is probably a reflection of not knowing the girlfriend and feeling uncomfortable around her. Still, it's something you have to check out.

When You Have a New Relationship

Introducing the new love of your life to your children can be a big win or a spectacular failure. In the beginning, temper your enthusiasm and understand just how emotionally challenging this is for your children. Love and acceptance cannot be forced. Give your children and your new partner time to get to know each other. A few important ground rules will help steer you toward success:

TIMING IS EVERYTHING

Wait until you are fairly certain the relationship will last a while before you introduce your new partner to your children. Involving them in every date can be confusing. Children may bond with each person and then grieve when they go away. Or they may show their discomfort by acting rude and obnoxious, which isn't pleasant for anyone.

TELL YOUR CO-PARENT

Once you are divorced, a great many details about your private life are no longer your former spouse's concern. However, when you bring another person into your children's lives, it is the other parent's business. Give your co-parent the courtesy of advance notification. It's smart to enlist his or her support, if possible. He or she can help your children accept your new partner, or they can sabotage your efforts.

TAKE BABY STEPS

Make the first few meetings between your children and your new partner short and informal. Go for frozen yogurt or hit the movie theater together. Afterward, go your separate ways so you have time alone with your children. Gradually work up to spending longer stretches of time with your kids and your new partner. If your new partner also has children, resist the temptation to prematurely roll everyone into one big happy family. Slow and steady is the way to go.

BE SENSITIVE ABOUT SEXUALITY

Give thought to how you want to introduce your children to the sexual aspects of your new relationship. Early on you may decide to limit kissing and hugging in front of your children. It's usually quite uncomfortable for them, and they may let you know with eye rolls and complaints. Pay attention to those cues. You will also have to decide when or if you want to spend the night together when your children are with you. This is an individual choice; there's no right or wrong decision. Preparing your children ahead of time will ensure a more positive reception. Let your children know when someone will be spending the night with you. You may want to say that your bedroom door will be closed and if they need you, please knock. Some parents put a lock on the door to ensure their privacy.

My Child Doesn't Like My New Partner

You may be completely smitten and happily fantasizing about creating the life of your dreams with your new love. And then your child bursts the bubble. He doesn't like your boyfriend. Or she doesn't want a "new mother." How do you handle it?

First, remember that most children hold out hope that their parents will get back together even long after the divorce is finalized. Your new relationship squashes that fantasy and makes it clear that the wished-for reconciliation isn't going to happen. Give your child time to mourn that loss and get acclimated to a new vision of the future.

Next, listen with compassion to your child's objections to your new partner. He may feel defensive of his other parent or disloyal if he likes your new partner. She may miss one-on-one time with you, feeling pushed out or replaced. Perhaps your new partner is coming on too strong, forcing a relationship before children are ready, or acting like a parent, which children hate. Once you are able to understand the reasons behind your child's dislike, it's much easier to address them. Reassure your children that you aren't trying to replace their other parent and explain that your new partner can fill a different, complementary role in your child's life.

Finally, recognize that introducing a new adult into the family is an awkward and sometimes painful experience for children. They are used to seeing their parents together and are likely still grieving the loss of family as they knew it. Give them time. When children say they don't like something, it can simply mean it's new or unfamiliar. Keep talking and listening. Observe the interactions between your children and your new partner with an open mind, always being alert to keeping your children emotionally and physically safe. Don't push your children into a new family before they're ready.

In the end, you, not your children, get to make the decision about your relationship. Give children a voice but not a vote. Don't ask if you should stay with a particular person, or let children choose whom you marry. It is never in their best interests to have that kind of power over adult lives.

Bumps on the Road to a Stepfamily

*K*irsten's divorce was painful, marked by ongoing conflict with her children's father. When he moved out of the area for work, she was frankly relieved. Co-parenting with him had been a nightmare. Her two boys missed their father terribly, though, especially because his attempts to connect with them were sporadic. For them, it seemed as if he'd dropped off the face of the earth.

In contrast, Jared's divorce was quite amicable. He and his former wife Lisa met monthly for co-parenting meetings and occasionally attended their children's events together. Jared harbored hopes of reconciling and was devastated when Lisa announced her engagement to one of his good friends.

Jared and Kirsten knew each other from Cub Scouts, where their sons were best friends. The boys were overjoyed when their parents began dating. Over the next year, the two families spent more and more time together. Kirsten's boys found a father figure in Jared and bloomed under his attention. Jared's son and daughter were less happy with Kirsten. They were already reeling from their mother's upcoming marriage and didn't want to deal with another newcomer.

Fortunately for the children, Kirsten, Jared, and Lisa understood the difficulties their children faced with these new relationships and were determined to focus on their children's needs. Individually and together, they talked and listened with their children. Jared and Lisa continued monthly co-parenting meetings, and occasionally Kirsten joined them when appropriate.

Kirsten and Lisa developed a relationship based on respect for each other as parents. They weren't friends—more like colleagues or business partners. They were able to share information, attend children's events, and offer occasional parenting backup.

Two years after they started dating, Kirsten and Jared decided to get married. They planned a lovely ceremony that included their four children, bought a house together, and thought they'd done everything they could to keep their children's needs at the forefront.

Jared laughingly described the wedding day like this: "Kirsten looked absolutely gorgeous and I was so happy to be marrying her. I really thought we'd pulled this stepfamily thing off. I guess it was a little premature. My daughter Ella ❯

couldn't stop crying. In fact, we had to plead with her to even enter the church. After the ceremony, when we turned to face the congregation, it was as if our children had been taken over by evil spirits. All four had tears running down their cheeks and sadness etched across their faces. Our two youngest sons—the ones who were best friends from Scouts—started arguing with each other as we walked out of the church. For the next two years, they stopped being friends. Our children's reactions were overwhelming, disappointing, and humbling. We realized again how complicated and difficult our new relationships are for them."

These children were lucky to have open and compassionate adults to guide them. Gradually, with a great deal of talking and listening, the children settled contentedly into both of their new families.

Conclusion

You're on your way to creating a full, happy life for yourself and your children. As I hope you've discovered from this book, divorce doesn't have to be the nightmare our culture sometimes makes it out to be. You can still be the great parent you've always strived to be and your children can have a joyful childhood they look back on with much fondness. Your path will not always be smooth, but believe me, slow and steady will get you where you want to go.

As you work through your divorce, always be mindful of the three main things your children need to thrive: involved, loving parents who are willing to be emotionally and physically present for them; the freedom and opportunity to love each of you without ever feeling disloyal to the other; and protection from destructive conflict.

If you choose to be an emotion coach for your children, and I hope you do, you will be setting them up for rich and satisfying lives. Many opportunities will arise that can become teachable moments in which you model how to effectively express and understand feelings. Think of how they will grow from this guidance!

I've given you a great deal to think about and perhaps at a time when you are already feeling overwhelmed. Don't worry. Just take one small suggestion and give it a try. Then try another when you feel ready. There's no rush. Simply focus on loving your children and creating a stable home for them.

More than anything, I hope that as you read this book you felt supported and encouraged to do what your children need. Here's to no more worries that keep you awake into the wee hours of the morning. You can do this. I know you can.

As I wrote this book, I recalled an afternoon long ago when my then six-year-old son helped his father and me load his dad's furniture into a truck. One of my son's neighborhood friends came over and in a very worried voice asked, "Are you moving?" My son casually replied, "No, we're just divorcing." For him it wasn't a big, scary event because his dad and I did our best to make it as easy as possible for him. Ultimately, our divorce was only one part of his life, not the traumatic main event. I'm proud to say he's turned out to be a kind, generous, and magnificent man and a wonderful father. And my heartfelt wish is the same for your children.

References

Emery, Robert. *The Truth about Children and Divorce.*
New York: Viking, 2004.

Goleman, Daniel. *Emotional Intelligence,* 10th ed. New York:
Random House Publishing Group, 2006.

Gottman, John. *Raising an Emotionally Intelligent Child.*
With Joan DeClaire. New York: Simon & Schuster, 1997.

The National Child Traumatic Stress Network. "How Does
Domestic Violence Affect Children?" December 2014. Accessed
September 19, 2015. www.nctsn.org/sites/default/files/assets
/pdfs/childrenanddv_factsheetseries_complete.pdf

Pedro-Carroll, JoAnne. *Putting Children First: Proven Parenting
Strategies for Helping Children Thrive Through Divorce.*
New York: Avery, 2010.

Syvertsen, A. K., E. Roehlkepartain, and P. C. Scales.
"Key findings from The American Family Assets Study."
Minneapolis, MN: Search Institute, 2012.

Resources

BOOKS

Books about parenting and parenting after divorce are plentiful. These are some of my favorites.

Deal, Ron. *Dating and the Single Parent*. Bloomington, MN: Bethany House Publishers, 2012.

Emery, Robert. *The Truth about Children and Divorce*. New York: Viking, 2004.

Faber, Adele, and Elaine Mazlish. *How to Talk So Kids Will Listen & Listen So Kids Will Talk*. rev. ed. 2012; repr., New York: Scribner, 1980.

Goleman, Daniel. *Emotional Intelligence,* 10th ed. New York: Random House Publishing Group, 2006.

Gottman, John. *Raising an Emotionally Intelligent Child*. With Joan DeClaire. New York: Simon & Schuster, 1997.

McBride, Jean. *Encouraging Words for New Stepmothers*. Fort Collins, CO: CDR Press, 2001.

Pedro-Carroll, JoAnne. *Putting Children First: Proven Parenting Strategies for Helping Children Thrive Through Divorce*. New York: Avery, 2010.

Ricci, Isolina. *Mom's House, Dad's House: Making Two Homes for Your Child*. New York: Touchstone, 1997.

Siegel, Daniel J., and Tina Payne Bryson. *The Whole-Brain Child: 12 Revolutionary Strategies to Nurture Your Child's Developing Mind*. New York: Bantam Books, 2012.

WEBSITES

There is an ever-changing universe of information available on the Internet. Some sites stand the test of time while others don't last. Start here for good resources.

uptoparents.org A free, confidential, interactive website for divorcing and divorced parents.

ourfamilywizard.com Our Family Wizard gives parents a way to share messages, schedules, and other parenting information. It offers a place to keep accurate records to help eliminate the "he said/she said" that sometimes happens in divorce.

divorcehelpforparents.com My website for divorced parents offers a wealth of common sense, research-based tips, and strategies.

ORGANIZATIONS & EXPERTS

National Stepfamily Resource Center
stepfamilies.info

Smart Stepfamilies
smartstepfamilies.com

Colorado Center for Life Changes
coloradocenterforlifechanges.com

Index

Acknowledgments

Divorced parents are some of the bravest people I know. I am so very grateful and honored to have shared the journey with many of you. Together, we are creating a new, more child- and family-friendly paradigm for divorce.

A huge and heartfelt thank you goes to my amazing supportive friends and family who brought soup and encouragement as I hunkered down to write. Many blessings to the wonderful team at Callisto Media who first thought of this book and then so beautifully helped me bring it to life. And to R.W.—You've always had my back and that means the world to me.